CW00486532

I'm Alright…
I'm Only Hurting.

Pippa Rafael

Faithbuilders
Publishing UK

© Pippa Rafael 2021

Faithbuilders Publishing
United Kingdom

ISBN: 978-1-913181-77-2

All rights reserved. No Part of this Publication may be reproduced, stored in a retrieval system, or transmitted in any form or by any means without the prior permission of the publisher.

British Library Cataloguing in Publication Data. A catalogue record for this book is available from the British Library

Formatted by Faithbuilders Publishing
Cover design by Ruth Holland
Printed in the United Kingdom

Contents

Dedication

I dedicate this book to my husband Geoff, for his patience and love. He remains the one whose arms are always there without reserve.

Also to Rob and Ann, who have tirelessly stood by me with unconditional love and support, believing for the best in the worst of times.

Without these special friends my voice would have never been heard and I wouldn't have been able to confront and let go of the pain of my past.

Endorsements

Violence, defilement, abuse and sexual molestation are experiences and descriptions that are distasteful and repulsive for any human being to encounter. However, when that person is a child of six years old, the revulsion is so intense that its effect on the mind and spirit of the hearer sharpens the senses and the conscience to scream that justice must be upheld, and that any and every perpetrator must be brought to account for their evil actions.

My friend Pippa has carried a secret of the heaviest weight for over forty years, although this secret was known by those close to the perpetrator! Her silent suffering, guilt and hidden pain have caused physical and mental torment, and, had it not been for the reality of a spiritual walk with Christ, her demise would be inevitable. Now, after the passing of her mother, she is able to tell her story in full, from a place of defilement and continual torment to one of freedom and liberation.

I personally understand Pippa's situation as I run a children's centre in Ghana called the Koby Foundation, a registered charity that cares for, feeds and educates disadvantaged and abused children.

Marie Willis

This is a book that was never meant to be written, yet it has become one that was necessary to write! In places it is not an easy read, partly because of Pippa's life threatening, long term, chronic physical illness, but also the horrible darkness of sexual abuse, which overshadowed the life of this six year old girl into her teenage years almost destroying her. Therefore, be prepared to be stunned for two reasons: the iniquitous and malevolent sexual abuse of an innocent and vulnerable little girl by a close relative, and also the heartfelt response of Pippa as she writes with courage and tenacity, undergirded by a graceful sensitivity and vulnerability which percolates through the deep pain.

There have been years of emotional, mental and physical pain, which never go away. You cannot bury your problems dead, you just push them further down. Pippa would agree that these traumatic wounds have a habit of catching you unaware, as certain circumstances can trigger a reaction causing further pain.

Pippa writes her story with honesty and discretion, and you will see that this has only become possible because of her deep faith in a caring and loving Heavenly Father. 'Kintsugi,' is a golden repair in the very old Japanese art of restoring broken pottery, using gold which makes the item become more beautiful than it was before it was broken. The repair is illuminated by the gold, and the flaws seem to be embraced by the gold. For Pippa, it is as though she is continually being embraced by God in the process of her recovery.

Pippa is a work in progress; so much has happened and so much has wonderfully changed. As she says in the epilogue, she is now wearing new shoes, but is bedding them in! We are thankful to God.

Rev Steve Hepden MTh

Introduction

Our lives can appear to be in order and that's what people want us to believe. But what happens when trauma from childhood takes on a life of its own and the little person inside begins to control the big person on the outside?

This book is my story. It is very honest and, at times, uninhibited but shows my journey and how I learnt to listen to that little person and understand her and comfort her, until she reached a place where she could hold hands with the adult and walk forward: healed, whole and with purpose.

This is a journey with Jesus from early childhood, taking the reader through all the questions, failures, fears, challenges and disappointments that trauma and abuse imprints upon the soul and helping us to see that there is always hope and that healing is always available.

Chapter One
No Place like Home

The rain had just been pouring down the window again, every drop falling into the next. I loved watching it run down and listening to the sound of it hitting the glass. It was such a good feeling to be sitting with my quilt wrapped around me, feeling warm and safe at home. Through the window, I could hear faint voices of children playing in the playground at the school nearby. Every morning, Mummy always swung the windows wide for fresh air... rain or shine!

For me, it was another day not at school because of my breathing problems but I never really thought too much about it as it had been like this for as long as I could remember. My tiny pink tablets, which helped control my breathing, tasted really nice so, when no one was looking, I crunched on a handful, leaving me incredibly shaky and sleepy. Mummy didn't seem to notice, and I didn't say anything because I felt lighter and less anxious about the difficulty of breathing.

None of this mattered anyway as all I could think about was getting out my pencil case and my pencils to draw, copying every face I saw! I drew every animal picture we had around the house and every face in the newspaper. "One day, I will be a brilliant portrait artist," I used to say to myself. Mummy loved my attempts and enthusiastically provided me with a constant supply of new drawing pads and pencils... and a chocolate bar! She would cut it in half and say, "Half now, half later!" I never understood that. Maybe that's why I now insist on eating two bars every time!

It seemed like I spent more days home than at school but that was just how I liked it. Home was my safe place with Mummy, Daddy and my brother, Joey.

Joey was five years older than me and I seemed to be waiting ages for him to come home every time he went out. I loved him so much and looked up to him.

"Dan Dan, where are you?" he would shout when he ran through the door. I still don't know why he called me a boy's name but, somehow, I liked it anyway. "Come on, let's throw the monkey!!!" My favourite game!

We started at one end of the room and threw the monkey to the other side, and then a frantic clambering pursuit began to see who would get to it first. It sounds like a straightforward task, but we would do anything to stop each other grabbing it! The room was ten feet square and full of furniture to negotiate and by the time the winner screamed, "I've got it!!!", we were both completely dishevelled with hair matted together, clothes pulled to fit the next size up, totally out-of-breath and exhausted!

"Joey!" my mum would shout. "Be calm! Your sister can't run around today; she had another bad attack in the night!" He would come and ruffle my hair and go to his bedroom and play with his marbles that I could soon hear hitting the skirting boards with force.

Daddy was my prince and that's what I called him. He got kissed a thousand times a day and I took great pleasure in wetting his shiny silver hair and standing it up on end to a sharp point as he said, "That's Imperial Leather for you!" He was in his fifties when I was born, and everyone thought he was my grandad at school, but it made absolutely no difference to me. I felt proud that he was my Daddy. He wore a crisp shirt and tie every day...with one exception. When he was up pruning the trees, he would roll his sleeves back and not wear his tie!

I followed him everywhere! He was my world.

His stamp collection filled my long hours at home as we soaked off the stamps and put them all in order. We had a routine every day that started with the stamps, then Daddy would lay the saxophone out after making sure the reed was just right, lift the lid on the piano, gently place his piano accordion down and check that the violin was in tune. Everything was ready for us to entertain ourselves for the rest of the evening! Three instruments, two people, only one who could play any of them!

He would produce a Bounty bar from some hidden place and we would smile a knowingly sneaky smile at each other that said, "Mummy doesn't know about this one!" And she wouldn't!

"Daddy can we start now? I will sing and you can play!"

Daddy was the calmest, gentlest person I knew. He had a deep love for God and his longing to see His glory and power oozed from him. "Pippa, you can know Him and He will be the closest friend you will ever have," he would say. I knew it to be true because I could see it in Daddy. Every time he spoke about Jesus, his face lit up and he became animated and excited - not something Daddy did normally as his shyness kept him quite subdued. As he prayed and knelt over his bed, I would climb onto his back and curl up and rest my head on the back of his head. He would pray under his breath with such love to Jesus and with such faith. Being on Daddy's back was my favourite place in the whole world.

The night times were difficult in our house as my breathing problems were worse at night. The kettle was on permanent boil to fill the bedroom with steam. Dr Buckler had said it would ease things for me. Mummy had to mop the walls down in the mornings as the condensation had dripped down them all night. She always said, "Thank goodness it's woodchip paper!" Everyone had woodchip. It was everywhere!

The lights were on and off all night. Mummy would sleep sitting up in my bed and hold me up against her chest as lying down was impossible for me because of my breathing. To the household's annoyance, I also had a barking cough which accompanied the asthma, keeping everyone awake.

"Mummy, I don't want to go to school tomorrow!"

They were always my first words after I'd come through an attack. Why would I want to be there? I felt tired and unwell and the eczema on my body was so irritating. To make matters worse, everybody laughed at me scratching so much.

Every third night, Mummy wrapped me up in tar bandages which was like being dipped in dark treacle and then rolled up.

"Why has she got bandages on and smells funny?" the kids in my class whispered to each other... a little too loudly so I could hear them.

I guess I did smell funny, but I was glad my legs were covered up because most of the time they were bleeding and so sore, so it was nice to hide behind the white strips. 'Scabby' was my name in primary school and the kids gave me a wide berth to avoid 'catching it'.

"Of course you can stay at home," my mum always answered. It was always a relief as I hated being away all day and I didn't understand what the teacher was saying as I'd missed so much class time.

"What would you like for tea?" Mummy always asked, supposedly, to cheer me up after a bad night. I always thought that it was a silly question because she cooked the same meal five or six nights in a row, so it was almost guaranteed what was on the menu. I didn't care what was for tea - although a Fray Bentos steak-and-kidney pudding always put a smile on my face. Unfortunately, they were served sparingly as she always said they were full of rubbish. All that mattered to me was that I was at home and Mummy was close by.

Sundays were a special day in our house and we always went to church. Joey and I were allowed a piece of paper and a pencil to doodle with during the preach: he drew hangman and noughts and crosses whereas I, on the other hand, drew the preacher and always drew them with a big nose or ugly smile because they always seemed so serious.

The organist was called Mrs. Hathpot. She had a great big pink hat with matching jacket and skirt, and she pumped the pedals of the organ so hard that her calves were gigantic. I guess that riding her bike furiously round the village also added to their size. Mummy always told me to stop staring during the hymn singing, which made me all the more curious. Mummy wore a hat, too, but hers was like a big badger and it fascinated me as to why you would put an animal on your head!

"RON!" my mum shrieked at the top of her voice, one peaceful Sunday afternoon. We all ran to the window to see her poking a brush up the tree to get her treasured hat down. Daddy thought it would be really funny to sit it up high on top of the tree. If anyone else had seen it, they would have grabbed their rifle and shot it dead... had they got one, of course! He had a very mischievous sense of humour and Joey and I loved it.

Mummy saw the funny side too, eventually. However, her humour was more on the daft side, and she could get quite some mileage out of a funny situation. She laughed so infectiously, holding her sides, while Daddy, who thought she had gone on for far too long, would stand up calmly and leave the room with a deep sigh. That was the extent of his anger!

There was a peace in our home and, although my health problems brought challenges, Mummy and Daddy always seemed happy and Mummy always reminded me to think of buttercups and daisies when I felt sad. I never could understand the connection (plus I didn't even like flowers), but it was said in such a kind way that it helped for now.

The sad times were a constant recurrence for me and their impact appeared to go completely unnoticed. "Please don't make me go!" Tears would roll down my face but I knew I had to. Yet another asthma attack that couldn't be stabilised.

"Yes, you have to go to hospital," Mummy would say. "You will be home soon!" But I always wondered if I would ever come home. Dr Buckler, who visited every third night during the night, was so gently-spoken with a sad but kind look on his face and always used to say, "The sooner you go, the sooner you will be home." At that point, he left the room to have another 'private chat'! They thought I couldn't hear but it wasn't new news. I'd heard him say it so many times before: "If she doesn't go now, we could lose her."

Mummy and Daddy would put me in the ambulance and wave me off, always looking so sad. I was scared but felt like I had to be strong despite being so small. As l travelled, everyone around seemed so uneasy and the blue lights flashed away. I wished that Mummy could have come but I accepted that it was what it was and that I had to be brave!

The arrival at hospital was always a fearful time and the doctors and nurses ran round putting my mask on, drips up, and taking blood gases from my arteries... sometimes in my wrist but, if it was proving difficult, they quickly took it from my groin as time was of the essence. This pain was on a different level from venous blood tests and hurt beyond belief.

My fluffy pink dressing gown was taken off and I was stripped naked and often sat with nothing on for a while until examinations were done and someone thought to dress me. Time in there went so slowly and I felt so alone. It sometimes took hours to, as they called it, 'stabilise' me. I cried very quietly for my mummy until I fell asleep.

The hours and days passed by and I learnt to just lie still and stare at the ceiling and as I was zipped up in an oxygen tent in a side room, it felt like I was far away from everyone. It became a regular occurrence and as I lay very still, I switched off my emotion and went into my own world, drifting away and not feeling anything. I loved to pretend I was a white piece of paper with no marks on it at all: just something that looked like nothing and no one would even notice. It made everything so easy when it was time for more invasive tests that hurt and examinations by doctors that scared me.

The one person that I didn't cut myself off from was Jesus. I told Him everything and we would lie on the bed together. I knew that He knew what I was thinking and feeling. Daddy had made sure I understood that.

Daddy never came to the hospital, probably because he was painfully shy and he seemed to struggle around people. He didn't really go out anywhere other than church. Mummy, on the other hand, was always standing and waiting for the moment that the stern ward sister opened the doors and declared visiting, 'Open'. She only stayed an hour a day as that was the rule in the 1970s. I was always eager to see what she had in her neatly-packed bag. Mummy always arrived with a treat which usually consisted of a nice new drawing pad and pencils or felt tips and some chopped-up fruit, "For goodness," she said! I knew that if Daddy had come, he would have produced a Bounty bar which would have been much more appreciated!

I was admitted to the cardiac/respiratory ward rather than the children's ward as there needed to be specialist breathing equipment and drugs readily available. Over the years, I had learnt to recognise the signs that another death had just occurred on the ward. A rapid pull of all the curtains all the way down the ward and all the doors closing abruptly signalled for us all to stay in bed.

Many a time, I watched the person in the next bed or opposite take their last breath and as I got older, I would go to them, stroke their hands and say it was all ok and pray for them. Then, pulling my drip behind me, I would walk over to the desk to tell the nurse that someone had just died.

Mr Jenkins had struggled to breathe for days. I watched him so closely and understood how he struggled as my lungs were just as fragile. It took three days for him to die! I felt like I knew his pain and I prayed, "Oh Lord, look after him!" I was just six, yet it was something that had become normal and I didn't realise it wasn't a normal occurrence for other children.

At school, I would tell them about 'The Tin' and how the person was dropped in with a THUD and wheeled away.

The experiences in hospital had started to embed in me a sense of loneliness and I increasingly found it difficult to express what I was thinking and especially what I was feeling. Talking about these experiences and feelings was something I did just to Jesus, especially if it was something upsetting or frightening.

Back home was my haven, and I became increasingly insecure, longing to stay at home where I felt so loved and safe.

"Come on, climb up," Daddy would say. It was our nightly routine before bed. One trip round the garden on Daddy's back, sometimes dodging the rain, and then we would kneel to pray at the side of my bed as my love grew and deepened for Jesus.

Daddy had said, "He will become your closest friend!" He was so right!

Chapter Two
Buttercups and Daisies

The weekend had arrived and that meant one thing... a 'Company Tea'! That's what my mummy called them, anyway. She had spent the last few days baking her famous coffee cake and lemon drizzle slab cake and cleaning the house as if we were moving or inviting the Queen to come and stay. We were all strictly warned not to go near the cakes but, when she wasn't looking, I would lift the top layer and frantically scoop out a chunk of buttercream and place the lid back down, checking that it looked like it was in its original condition.

Company Teas were on a Saturday afternoon, and I marvelled at the lengths my mummy would go to in order to have her salad just so! She laid every salad item with precision and had an egg-slicer which sliced with such accuracy. When she wasn't slicing eggs, I pretended to play it like a harp. Mum was not pleased at all as it was for 'eggs and eggs alone', as she would say in a firm tone.

I couldn't wait for Uncle Ray and Auntie Iris to arrive. They always unloaded a bag full of what my mummy thought were treats...but who could get excited about a tin of red salmon and some home-pickled onions? There were also usually a couple of jars of honey and a great big bag of green beans which we seemed to be stringing and slicing for days. There it was! MY gift! A bag of butterscotch and more drawing things. Yay! I was on cloud nine.

Uncle Ray and Auntie Iris were my favourite auntie and uncle. I was the only girl on that side of the family, so they said I was special. And they made me feel it, too. I'd sit for hours on Uncle Ray's knee. He always wore a thick, green knitted jumper

19

that had wooden buttons, and a tie that I never thought matched. Not like my daddy, who everyone said looked like the captain of a ship.

Auntie Iris was gentle and spoke with such kindness... when she could get a word in, that is, because Uncle Ray 'took the chair'. That's what Mummy always said after he'd left. Happy Saturdays and sunshine Sundays; that's how they felt to me.

It was the summer holidays, and I was six. Daddy would get a big tin bath out and fill it with water for me to play in. In no time at all, it was full of grass and mud at the bottom but that made no difference to me. I was too excited! My best friend, Emmy, came round from next door and we sat in it all afternoon with our umbrellas up, singing our hearts out.

I hadn't realised at this point but, now the summer holidays were here, Mummy and Daddy had decided to let me go and stay for two weeks with my other uncle and auntie down south, in Watford. Auntie Glenda and Uncle Ivan. Auntie was my mum's sister, and I knew that Mummy loved her very much. Auntie Glenda had some troubles, Mummy said, and I was told to always be kind to her. That wasn't hard because Auntie was always really kind to me and interested in my drawings and said how good they were. Mummy had to tell me to stop showing off because when they came to visit, Auntie would ask to see my work as soon as she walked through the door and Uncle Ivan got me to show him all my gymnastic moves.

Even though Uncle Ivan watched me perform, I didn't feel the same towards him as my lovely Uncle Ray. Daddy said he was a very clever man and built huge buildings, but I realised early on that he had a lot to say for himself and, in my mind, he was a big show-off, not like my talkative Uncle Ray. He couldn't stop talking but always said things in a way that made me like him. He was a man that loved God and he would tell us about all the funny things that happened in the churches he preached in. Uncle Ivan, on the other hand, seemed to constantly give out advice and his opinions as if they were fact.

20

To my surprise, Mummy told me that she'd been chatting to Uncle Ivan and that they had arranged for me to go and stay with them for a couple of weeks. I didn't really want to go because I didn't want to leave Mummy and Daddy, but I didn't seem to be able to tell them. I thought that they would be upset with me because it might upset Auntie... and how could I say that I was scared? I hadn't wanted them to know how frightened I often felt away from home.

Uncle Ivan came to pick me up. He said it was a really long way and, as it was so hot in the car, I was just to wear my vest and shorts. Mummy had all my best dresses packed so neatly and she told me to look smart all the time. The shorts and vest idea sounded good to me! With a 'not-best-pleased' look, Mummy relented this once and we were on our way.

The journey was so long, and Uncle Ivan didn't say much as we travelled down. How I wished that Auntie Glenda had come to pick me up, too. My chest was tight because Uncle Ivan had the window down as it was so hot. Mummy always kept it up on our journeys, saying, "Let's keep the pollen out and the clean air in."

Finally, we arrived... and there she was! Auntie ran up the steps and scooped me up in her arms. I was so pleased to see her. A little nervousness was beginning to set in as I was so far from home, and it was a completely new environment which always made me want Mummy and to be at home.

"Come on, Pippa. I've cooked a special tea for you!"

We clambered down the really long stone steps with my big shiny brown suitcase and bags of things for Auntie that Mummy had sent as a treat. There were fifteen steps in all. In the following two weeks, I repeatedly counted them and wished so many times that it was time to go up them and go home for good.

It was the summer of 1976, and we were in the middle of a heatwave. Uncle Ivan was complaining about the hosepipe ban.

I didn't really understand what that meant but it must have been a big deal because everyone was talking about it.

Uncle Ivan wore just his shorts for most of that holiday. Most people would have been doing the same, but not my Daddy. He still wore his smart trousers and shirt, although he did remove his tie a couple of times because he was clearly suffering with the heat.

The first day at their house was just an ordinary day, but that's what I liked. As long as I wasn't on my own and I could see Auntie, I felt as safe as I could, being away from home. Auntie said, "Let's just settle you in and we will do some exciting things over the next couple of days."

I had the little back bedroom and in it was a bed with a pink frilly quilt-cover on. Next to the bed was a chair with a little dolly sitting crossed-legged. This little doll became my best friend, and after a few cuddles I was surprised to see that when you turned her round, she had another face on the back! This face was very sad. I stared at it for a while and decided I preferred the happy face. I was so glad to share my room with her because I hadn't brought my dolly from home or my monkey that stood two feet tall and usually they went everywhere with me. The room was bright but quite bare and on the back of the door were lots of ties and belts. I guessed that they were Uncle Ivan's.

"Tea time!" shouted Auntie. I ran downstairs and could smell what Mummy described as 'a wholesome cooked meal'.

While Auntie Glenda washed up and tidied the kitchen, Uncle Ivan sat reading the newspaper, then put it down and flicked the telly on. I had noticed all the hairs on his legs and thought that only monkeys had hairs like that. I'm sure it was exaggerated in my mind, but I had no comparison as my daddy NEVER showed his legs. My mummy said that it was because he was a gentleman.

I ran over and sat down next to Uncle Ivan and started to stroke his hairs. It made me laugh and he seemed perfectly happy for me to do it. The windows were wide open and there was no breeze. It was a humid evening, and I just had my shorts and a little vest on. In the hallway, the phone began to ring. "Ivan, answer that," shouted Auntie.

A few minutes later, I ran through to the hallway to Uncle who was sitting on the chair of the telephone table which was an all-in-one piece of furniture. He was talking to my cousin Stanley, his son. He signalled for me to come to him, then reached over and pulled me close. I liked being cuddled as my daddy always held me close and made me feel safe.

Within a few minutes, this felt different. Uncle Ivan slowly wedged my legs apart and put his hand on top of my shorts! Everything inside me went rigid and I felt very unsure of what was happening. Something didn't feel right. It must be ok, though, because it's my Uncle Ivan. Maybe he doesn't realise it's a funny place. Maybe he didn't mean to. Maybe he's distracted whilst talking to Stanley.

He then forced his hand down my shorts on top of my pants. "No!" I screamed inside. I didn't like it, but it must be ok. Then his hand went into my pants! I turned my head and looked up into his face, hoping he could see that I was very scared and confused. He just continued to talk to Stanley as though absolutely nothing was happening. The conversation about central heating and copper piping went on and on.

Suddenly, I entered a different world. It made no sense, and I didn't seem to be able to say, "I don't like it!" He put his feet on mine so that I couldn't move. I wouldn't have anyway, because Mummy would have been so cross if I'd been naughty and disrespectful. My mind was racing, and nothing seemed to make sense. "Uncle Ray would never do this!" I thought to myself.

When he finally let me go, I wasn't sure what to do and ran to Auntie Glenda. She hadn't noticed that I was quieter than usual and was sticking to her like glue! My asthma wasn't too good, so she said I was to have an early night. "You've got extra pillows and you must come through to Uncle Ivan or me if you're poorly."

After my creaming regime for my eczema and taking my tablets, I was all tucked up in bed and cuddled my dolly, smiling-side up. I made sure of it. I didn't think any more about the 'strange touching' and tried to sleep but couldn't stop thinking about Mummy and Daddy. I talked to Jesus, and we smiled at each other. Well, I smiled at Him, and I waited, imagining Him smiling at me. I knew that He did. "Jesus, I love you. You are my best friend! I really don't want to be here. Please can I go home?" I slowly drifted off to sleep.

I was abruptly woken out of my sleep later that night as the bedroom door opened and a hand patted the bed covers. It was Uncle Ivan who was in his pyjamas. "Pippa. Pippa, wake up!" I sat up quickly because I thought something was wrong. "I have a really special present for you!" Oh boy! As you know, I liked presents! I'd become very accustomed to getting them after my attacks. I was so excited!

"Here it is!" he said, and he pushed his private parts up close to me. I was completely confused and felt very scared. How does a little girl respond to that? What should I do? I desperately tried to think. "Here... you hold it. It's a very special thing!"

It was something I'd never seen before. I hadn't even seen Daddy's legs or chest and Joey was old enough to want to be private. So Uncle Ivan's scary bits caused a repulsive feeling and I couldn't understand what was wrong. This definitely was not a nice present. I tried to say that I didn't want to hold it but the words wouldn't come out of my mouth. Is that what he wees with? What if he puts wee on me and what if this thing hurts me? I started to shake, and Uncle Ivan seemed to be cross with my huge lack of cooperation.

I scratched my legs. The eczema was sore and bleeding and I felt overwhelmed by the whole situation. Uncle Ivan tried to do more but I couldn't do what he seemed to want. I grabbed hold tight of my bed sheet and tried to hide underneath. Uncle Ivan put his hands under the sheet and put his hand down my body and touched me. I wriggled as much as I could to move away from him, but my body seemed to go numb and it wouldn't move. My whole being was screaming out, "Please come, Auntie Glenda. Please!"

She didn't!

After a while, he said, "Don't worry, Pippa. I will come back in the morning."

BACK IN THE MORNING!!!! The four worst words in the world! I crawled to the bottom of my bed and curled up into the tightest ball that I could. "Jesus, please help me!" I repeated, over and over again.

How can I stop him coming in the morning? This thought constantly whirled around in my head. It was no good. I couldn't do anything. I felt very helpless and strange and confused. I was used to being scared when I was in hospital, but Mummy always came to see me whenever she could and I knew my family loved me. This was different. Uncle Ivan loved me too and he watched me do my gymnastics, visited our house and talked so much to Mummy and Daddy. But what he had done didn't make sense. He was like a different man. He was quiet and calm, and his voice sounded nice but what he was doing wasn't. I cried, "Mummy, Daddy, Jesus, Mummy, Daddy, Jesus," all night. "Please come and get me!" I repeated under my breath. They seemed so very far away.

Uncle Ivan did come to see me in the morning. I heard the creak of the door and watched his hand come round to push it open. Something came up in my throat and I couldn't speak as the previous night's horror was replayed.

....

We stayed in most evenings and sat watching television. I'm not sure where Auntie Glenda was this particular night, but she didn't seem to be about. Uncle Ivan reached under the television to get out his *Dad's Army* collection. "This will do nicely," he said as he put the first one in the video slot.

Mummy and Daddy watched *Dad's Army*, too. I always enjoyed it because it was a bunch of ugly old men getting up to funny things that always made me laugh. I sat on the same settee as Uncle Ivan but as far away as possible. Oh, how I wished that the other chair wasn't covered in the day's washing pile!

"Come and sit next to me, Pippa."

I gulped, tried to shake my head to indicate 'no' and did a little nervous scratch. He pulled my arm and I quickly shuffled up next to him. I didn't want to be in trouble or to make him cross with me.

Dad's Army was playing away, and the house was otherwise silent. Uncle Ivan got my hand and rather determinedly put it down his trousers into his pants and put my hand on his private bits. My heart was racing, and I felt hot from the humid evening and hot from being nervous and scared. He put his hand on mine and continued to make me feel every part of him. After the second video started, it sort of became 'normal' as he sat completely relaxed and seemingly totally focused on the programme, laughing spontaneously at things. Did he realise what he was doing? How could he be smiling?

My face couldn't smile. My eyes were full of tears, and I was grinding my teeth together as quietly as I could so that Uncle Ivan wouldn't notice. My mind was racing, and I couldn't reconcile what was happening. My daddy wouldn't love me if he knew this was happening, I thought to myself. Mummy would be angry with me, too! I sunk into a state of acceptance and let my hand go limp. This caused Uncle Ivan to be annoyed and he pulled my hand out abruptly and, instead, put his hand straight into my pants.

"Please come, Mummy. Please help me, Jesus!" I prayed. It hurt and I felt sore. What was he doing? Doesn't he love me? He must love me...!

He didn't speak a word as he posted another video into the machine. It was great relief when he pulled his hand out. I wanted to get up and run but my body didn't seem like mine; it wouldn't do what I told it to. Uncle Ivan laid me across him and put his hand up my vest and located my nipples. He started to rub and rub, and this went on until he'd had enough. Didn't he know how sore they felt and the horrible detestable feeling it put into my body?

I'm not a nice little girl! My body is all wrong. I knew that from all the times it wouldn't work and I ended up in hospital. Maybe, I thought, that's why! Maybe my body is broken and he's just trying to fix it. From then on, because of this seemingly small act, I was deeply affected. Instantly, a repulsive feeling came in waves over me in a severe physical reaction whenever I accidentally caught my nipple on anything.

The videos ended and Uncle Ivan lost interest in me and got up to go to the bathroom. My mind was in a frenzy. Do I move from here? If I do, he might follow me. If I stay, he might come back! My pants were all dishevelled and I was too scared to move, frozen to the spot.

"Jesus, help me to stand up!" At that, I shuffled forwards and then ran as fast as I could to my bedroom to Dolly. She was lying on the bed with her sad face staring at me when I went in. I started to cry and tidied her hair. "It's ok, Dolly. Don't be sad. Jesus won't leave us."

It didn't take me long to realise that I was of no importance to Uncle Ivan unless he wanted to play the 'silent game'.

....

Auntie Glenda bustled in, all excited, after he'd gone to work, one day. "Come on, Pippa, get dressed. Let's go somewhere nice today."

It wasn't long before recent events slipped into the recesses of my mind. We went to the park and bought a pick-and-mix for 2p! Well, I was only allowed a 1p mix at home, so I thought that this was amazing! Double the amount of White Mice and Black Jacks!

"Come on. Let's get home; Uncle Ivan is taking us out for tea." I got dressed up in my best blue dress with little yellow flowers around the collar. My socks matched because Mummy always said, "I don't dress the windows for Marks and Spencer's for nothing!" She had a keen eye for colour and matching things together.

We arrived at a pub. This might have been of no consequence to anyone else, but I was worried that if Mummy knew, I would be in so much trouble. Mummy and Daddy said that those places were not for us and we must keep ourselves separate. I never really understood the term 'demon drink'.

Auntie Glenda insisted I had a bath when we got home. I hated having baths because of the huge white baths in the hospital in the middle of a massive room. And I didn't like taking my clothes off, either, because I always felt vulnerable. After tonight's bath, my fear of bath time was taken to another level... and understandably so.

Auntie Glenda was downstairs and said she would come up to help to dress and cream me when I was finished. Uncle Ivan walked into the bathroom and said, "Pippa, stand up." I went to get my towel, but he said in a firm voice, "No!" and he lifted me out of the bath. He told me he needed to see the eczema on my legs and to turn round. I really didn't want to and felt frightened after what had happened that previous night. Things went from bad to worse. After he was done, I was left in a distraught state, scrambling around the carpet and vomiting, curling up behind the toilet to try and stay safe. I didn't know what to do or how to sort things out. Eventually, I somehow found the strength to clean everything up.

The next short while was a blank and I found myself in my bedroom, frantically emptying my case of all my clothes and putting them all on in the desperate hope that Uncle Ivan wouldn't be able to get to me!

....

Where was Auntie Glenda? I'd had my cream on and I didn't want to show Uncle Ivan my eczema again! When Daddy creamed me, I wasn't scared, I could keep my pants on and I didn't have to lie down on the floor. "Please help me, Jesus!" In a anxious state, I rehearsed a little speech to Dolly over and over again, each time changing it a little to try to put the right words together to explain that I didn't like taking my clothes off and being 'looked at'! Eventually, I put Dolly down, sad face looking forward and said, "When I come back, you can smile."

Auntie Glenda had woodchip paper, too, and I poked at the wood that was in the paper, going round each piece slowly as I walked towards the door. My heart was racing, and I had decided that if I could try and make Uncle Ivan happy, then he wouldn't touch me. Maybe I could explain how I felt.

He had been having an afternoon nap and was lying on top of the covers on his bed. I poked my head around to see if he was awake. He looked over and called, "Come on in, Pippa."

I crept in slowly and spluttered, "Please don't...I mean, I don't want... erm... I don't like... my skin! I mean, don't look at my skin." In my six-year-old mind, I was being strong and I was being brave. "Do you want me to tickle your back and make you happy?" I said, my throat tightening. I thought that everything would be alright now: Uncle Ivan wouldn't hurt me if I made him happy! The thought of tickling him was my rationale that would make it all ok. But my plan failed miserably. I ended up with no clothes on again, feeling deeply upset with myself that my little strategy had made him touch me again.

It was all my fault and I had ugly skin and from that point on, I avoided looking in the mirror because the little girl looking back at me was ugly, stupid and cowardly.

....

The days rolled on and so did the sunshine. I sat, looking out of the window, counting the stone steps... and as I reached fifteen, my heart raced with excitement at the thought of going home. The sun was smiling but I didn't feel like smiling and I had problems with my new dolly friend. I couldn't hold her smiley-side-up anymore because of how sad I was. But if I held her sad-side up, I thought somebody would see and then I would be in so much trouble. By the time the holiday ended, I had hidden her under everything I could find in the room and stacked it all on top of her. She evoked in me so many emotions that, as a little girl, I couldn't handle.

Each day became a new day not for adventure but for what felt like imprisonment. I had no way of escape and the only thing I knew to do was to do everything that I was told: don't complain, keep respectful, don't tell anyone. I looked longingly at the telephone table at the bottom of the stairs. "Please, Mummy, ring me!" If only I'd had the strength to ask if I could ring her.

The final morning arrived. It was time to go home, and Auntie Glenda had packed up all my things, early. Dolly was sitting on the chair because I couldn't hide her anymore. Something strange happened as I was trying to say goodbye to her. I sat her with smiling face forward and an inner turmoil rose up so I quickly turned her round to show the sad face. NO, that's not right! I repeatedly turned her backwards and forwards, in an emotional state! My mind overloaded and I stood, shaking, against the wall, unable to move.

"Pippa, come downstairs!"

It was Uncle Ivan. I was rigid with fear and tried to shout back, "NO!" but it was like a mouse's squeal! Almost silent. What should I do? What will he do? I felt sick and my insides were trembling.

"Pippa, NOW!"

At that, I slowly made my way downstairs, I dared not disobey him because Mummy would be so mad and disappointed in me. As I walked into the room, Uncle Ivan fell on the floor, grabbed my ankles and started to cry. He asked how I felt. I dropped my head down and whispered that I felt scared and sad and embast. (I couldn't say embarrassed.)

Uncle Ivan whispered, "We have this secret, and NOBODY will ever know about it." He went on to explain why I should never talk about it, and he made me promise never to do so. I promised. I don't remember seeing Auntie Glenda around and she wasn't to come home with me. Finally, I climbed the last stone step and prayed to Jesus that I would never come back here again. It was the most frightening car journey I ever had. I was sitting in the back in my shorts and vest and my knees would not stop shaking. They knocked and knocked, and I was terrified that Uncle Ivan would see and do something to me like he had before. So, I sat with my hands cushioning my knees all the way home. Every time we stopped for petrol or to stretch our legs, it felt like my heart stopped, too.

Home was changed forever, now. I was changed and, somehow, no one seemed to notice. "Think of buttercups and daisies," Mummy would say whenever I looked sad or quiet. I desperately wanted her to ask me what was wrong, but I desperately didn't want her to ask, either! I just needed to be safe and to feel safe.

Chapter Three
Invisible Me

I'd had the most important experience I would ever have and found the best relationship I would ever keep around the time of 'the holiday'. Daddy was what some people describe as a 'Man of Faith'. He believed everything the Bible said and had an increasing desire to see miracles and people being healed. He would walk around the house reading books about great revivalists and healing ministers and would say, "Hey listen to this!" before proceeding to tell us of another amazing miracle that God had performed somewhere!

A healing evangelist was coming to town so, as you can imagine, Daddy and Mummy were quick off the mark to get me there, especially because of my need for healing from my brittle asthma. It was a summer's evening, and I was normally in bed by 7pm, so this was rather exciting. We chugged along in our big silver Vauxhall Victor estate. Daddy had done so many body retouches to it that I don't think there was much of the original bodywork left! We all excitedly arrived at the field, where an enormous tent was pitched and a huge flag was blowing in the breeze saying, 'Dick Saunders: Healing Evangelist! Meet with God Tonight!'

By the time the appeal was made, I knew that God was calling me to give my heart and life to Him. The organist began to play, and something welled up in me as I whispered in Mummy's ear, "I'm going forward." Before she could answer, I was on my way down to the front! That night, I understood the deep love of God for myself. It was no longer me walking in Mummy and Daddy's shadow, but I began my own relationship with Jesus. This would be my bedrock throughout my years growing up.

But after arriving home from my holiday 'down south', so much had changed. When I saw Mummy and Daddy, I was ecstatic and promised myself that I would never go away from home again. The usual nightly routine of trooping round the garden on Daddy's back before bed somehow felt different. As he carried me into my bedroom, I quickly jumped down. Something inside recoiled and I didn't want my Daddy anywhere near me!

My precious, adored daddy was different now! How could I trust him? What was he going to do? I froze and held my breath as he leaned forward to kiss me and tuck me in. It wasn't Daddy that had changed; it was me! From that night on, I made every excuse under the sun to get into bed without Daddy's assistance. But I missed him. I missed him so badly.

....

"Come on, Pippa, it's time for school." The night hadn't been too bad, so Mummy said I needed to go. I knew that the headmistress, Miss Rotchet, had questioned Mummy again about how much time I was absent from school and tomorrow was going to be the school medical. Mummy tried to reassure me: "It's ok; everyone has it. Don't worry." DON'T WORRY?!! I was PETRIFIED! What if they took my clothes off? What if Mummy wasn't there?

I had an internal melt down and froze to the spot! Mummy was busy spraying her hair at the hallway mirror and making sure that all the windows were closed before we set off. She didn't notice! When she came into my room to ask what I was doing, I couldn't answer. The fear of being examined was too much for me but Mummy hadn't noticed that something was very wrong. It was as if the trauma and chaos raging inside me was invisible.

I had my medical and imagined I was somewhere else. My body wasn't mine. It didn't belong to me; how could it? Mummy did stay when I saw the school doctor (who happened to be a man, which didn't help) and, much to her annoyance, I was rather uncooperative.

"Pippa, you were rude in there and when an adult speaks to you or asks you a question or tells you to do something, you must respond. Be respectful, Pippa!"

All I could say was, "Yes Mummy. I'm sorry. I love you!"

....

It was time for another 'Company Tea'. Uncle Ray and Auntie Iris were coming, and I couldn't wait. I wondered what they would bring me. As usual, they arrived with a bag full of 'boring' treats for Mummy and Daddy, but Joey and I got a tin of boiled sweets each! They were covered in fine icing sugar and every time I lifted the lid, a spray of fine powder puffed out. "A WHOLE tin full!" I said, under my breath. I quickly scuttled away and put them in my secret drawer in my chair before Mummy clocked them and took them away for rationing.

Uncle Ray called me over. "What's the matter, Pippa? Come and sit on my knee; let's have a big squeeze!" I stepped back and shook my head.

Mummy noticed and appeared to be cross, saying, "Pippa! Uncle Ray wants a cuddle; go and give him one!" She had a look that said, 'Do as you are told! NOW!!!' I went quickly as I didn't like to be in trouble.

Uncle Ray was, as usual, 'taking the chair'. He was in full flow, explaining about a funeral he'd conducted that had all gone terribly wrong. Meanwhile, I sat quietly on his lap. Normally, that would have been me for the next hour, but this time was different.

"What is he doing?" My mind was so shattered by what had happened weeks before with Uncle Ivan that Uncle Ray's touch

35

felt like it could be the same. He was stroking my tummy and inadvertently stroked over the top of my nipple. Something flipped inside and I jumped off his knee so abruptly that he stopped talking immediately and looked very concerned. "What's the matter, Pippa?"

I ran into my bedroom, grabbed my monkey and hid under the bed. Daddy came through to see what the matter was. Tears were rolling down my cheeks and Daddy's kind, concerned voice somehow coaxed me out. I couldn't tell him. I didn't even know what the matter was. All I knew was that being cuddled and stared and looked at was now something that I couldn't cope with. All my trust had been shattered and I had no idea who loved me!

....

I had a lovely bedroom and Mummy made sure it was all pretty and matching. As the breathing problems continued, I spent a lot of time in my room, lying on my bed and talking to Jesus. I had a children's Bible and lots of books about Him that I devoured, drawing every picture I thought worthy of copying. I felt so grown up when Mummy bought me a record player to listen to while I recovered during those long days. I was seven but felt eleven! It was as my music was playing about Jesus that I learnt to let go of my confusion and get some peace!

One particular day, my asthma started to worsen, and my allergies were raging so Dr Buckler came out to visit again. Mummy looked really tired and worried and, as the day wore on, I knew what the outcome would be. As Mummy held me, I watched her listening to Dr Buckler who had exhausted all his techniques and injections while trying to bring stability to my wracked body. He said those dreaded words: "We need to go now!" By this time, I was breathing very poorly, and I coughed relentlessly. Normally, I didn't feel scared as I was used to the restrictive feeling in my chest and not being able to breathe was like second nature, but I felt so ill and couldn't speak! Mummy had to do physio at times like this to try to dislodge the mounting phlegm.

I saw the blue lights appear from around the corner and knew that I had to leave Mummy again. This time, I didn't really care. I was seriously fighting for my life and needed help. Dr Buckler wasn't his normal calm self and didn't have his usual demeanour, being preoccupied with getting everything together as quickly as he could. He held me tightly and carried me into the ambulance. My stomach was in knots as Mummy helped to close the doors.

That night, I nearly died. Mummy, the consultant, several doctors and a room full of nurses all stood around my bed. Mummy was crying uncontrollably and tried to blow her nose on a saturated tissue that was strewn all over her lap. Apparently, I had been given all the lifesaving drugs they had and my body was in a cycle that seemed impossible to break. I remember the consultant saying, "There is nothing we can do now. Her lungs will either kick-in and respond or, I'm afraid to say, they most probably won't, and she will die."

Where was my Daddy? I need you Daddy!

I watched my mummy drifting away and I became so tired of the laboured breathing. "Jesus, I love you. Please help me!" I grabbed the bed covers out of desperation, trying to get some air in, then began to lose consciousness and wet myself.

The next thing I remember was waking up with multiple wires trailing from my body. Looking around frantically, I needed my mummy but she wasn't there! My bed was next to the nurse's station and monitors and alarms were going off. I was used to the hospital setting but this attack had been really serious. I wasn't on my usual ward and the nurses were too busy writing and looking at all the monitors to notice that I had recovered consciousness. My favourite pyjamas had been taken off and I was just under a sheet, tucked tightly under my arms. I heard the nurses saying, "Bay one, bed one," and, looking over at me, they all stared as a long conversation ensued.

Under my breath, I whispered, "Jesus, you know my name and I'm not a number to you." I lay with my hand open, imagining that Jesus was right there holding it tightly...and He was!

....

The next time I was admitted was when the eczema on my legs became badly infected...and the tar bandages didn't help. "We need to soak off these bandages, Pippa," said the kind nurse. They had got stuck and were so rigid with blood that I yelled as the nurse did her best to pull them away, bit by bit. I was made to stand naked. Fear gripped me and there was nothing I could do. I had completely lost my ability to speak up for myself... although I don't think I had ever been very good at it, anyway! I hated my body and I tried not to look at it. At home, Mummy had a big mirror in the lounge, and I always ran past it quickly, so I didn't get a glimpse of myself.

I was about eight years old and although the memories of the holiday with Uncle Ivan were fading, my overreactions to situations and people were not. Sometimes, I would imagine what it would be like to be a boy. If I were a boy, I wouldn't have to kiss people or sit on their lap. Hey, that's a thought! If I could be like a boy and act like a boy, I would be happy! I already felt ugly and didn't want people to look at me and Mummy always said how plain I was, so it must be true. That was it! I had a plan!

Excitedly, I started to put things in my pants so I would resemble a boy and to put tape on my doll between her legs. "Now she's safe," I smiled to myself before going on to stick a pretend-boy's tail on my monkey. This felt better but it had to all be secret so that Mummy, Daddy and Joey didn't know!

I carried on like this until it became hard to hide at school. No one at home noticed and I was glad they didn't because I was starting to feel shameful; if I'd have been caught, what would I have said? It was at times like these that my inner turmoil being invisible to others was an advantage.

38

Chapter Four
Silent Tears

The phone was ringing, and I shouted to Mummy in the garden as she watered the roses.

"Oh, hello," she said, into the phone. I listened intently as an exciting phone call unfolded. Mummy sounded pleased about something but, as usual, my health came into the conversation! "I appreciate your kindness but are you sure?" After a chat about whether or not I was well enough, Mummy put the phone down and shouted to me in my bedroom. "Pippa!"

Excitedly, I ran to see what the phone call was about. "Pippa, Uncle Ivan's son, Richard, wants you to be his bridesmaid!" My cousin Richard was loads older than me and I didn't really know him, but Mummy went on to explain how they felt sorry for me because of how ill l was and that I may never have another opportunity. I wondered if she said this because, in the past, I'd heard her saying that she didn't know how long I would live. I remember thinking that I wish I'd been picked because they thought I'd make a pretty bridesmaid or for some other nice reason, instead of pity. But nonetheless, I was ecstatic!

Everything was sorted for the wedding. I had a long, baby pink, off-the-shoulder bridesmaid dress that flowed to the floor! It was so lovely, and I'd never worn anything so grown up before! "Mummy, I won't have to say anything will I? And what if I make a mistake?"

I had little confidence in myself and the eczema on my legs was having a flare up. What if my legs were to bleed onto the dress? There were so many worries in my mind, and I began to be fearful about The Big Day and how I would cope if I couldn't breathe. Everyone will look at me! What if I'm unwell... and if my eczema is bad, what will Uncle Ivan say? Will he want to look at it? I don't want him near me and what if Mummy or Auntie Glenda are busy talking?

I sank myself into the only thing I knew and that was spending time with Jesus. As I lay on my bed listening to my records and singing under my breath, there was my dress hanging on the back of the door! Looking at it I said, "Jesus, I'm scared! I know you hold me in your hand, and I know you will never leave me, so please help me when I go to visit Uncle Ivan next week. Thank you that I'm a bridesmaid and please protect me from Uncle Ivan!" I was at peace. I opened my Bible and sunk myself into it. I knew His words were words of life to me.

I wished I could talk to Mummy or Daddy, but I couldn't... I'd made a promise! But why did this promise feel like it was burning a hole into my heart? It felt so right at the time to never tell anyone but now I felt so lonely and scared. "Jesus, I'm so glad I can tell you everything!"

We arrived at Uncle Ivan's house and there was so much hustle and bustle going on. People were everywhere, finalising things for the next day! The wedding day had finally arrived. It was a crisp February day, and the sunshine was shining brightly! The wedding seemed long and boring to me as all we seemed to do was stand and smile whilst feeling starving hungry and dying for a drink! The wedding came and went, and it all seemed a bit of a let-down. I had thought that being a bridesmaid was an amazing thing but soon realised that it was a day that probably adults enjoyed more!

The next few days were more memorable... but not for the right reasons.

During the visit, Auntie Glenda and Uncle Ivan suggested that we go to the zoo. I was so excited! All I wanted to see were the monkeys. My brother Joey and I loved monkeys! We would sit and discuss what sort of monkey we would have if we could, and we begged Mummy to let us have one. However, she said we'd need a special license... and she liked her curtains too much! "What a mess they'd make, swinging on them!" she'd say.

We had a great day at the zoo, but I wished that Joey could have been with me! He and Daddy had stayed at home: Daddy was too shy and Joey, who had no interest in weddings, opted to stay with him. How I soon wished I'd stayed with them! The joy of the day quickly vanished as Uncle Ivan seemed to go very quiet. Everyone had gone home after the wedding and there was just Uncle, Auntie and Mummy in the house. Somehow, Uncle Ivan managed to get me away from everyone and told me to go into the bathroom. I was a little older now and managed to muster up a "No, I don't want to," in rather a small voice, but an attempt, nevertheless!

"Turn round, let me see your eczema and lie down!" Where was Mummy? Inside, my heart was broken and the previous visit of four years before became more than just a memory. I felt myself close down and cried inside, gritting my teeth while desperately trying to hold back the tears.

"No one will ever know," I assured Uncle Ivan.

It was a great relief to finally arrive back home but, unfortunately, I brought the memories and anxiety with me. Dr Buckler said he was beginning to be concerned as I was rather subdued and that maybe the asthma was having a psychological effect on me. "Pippa, keep your chin up; think of buttercups and daisies," said Mummy. I always smiled at Mummy; she loved me so much and I wanted to please her. How could I ever tell her about how sad I was on the inside?

A few weeks later, the weather was damp, and the storage heaters had been on. Mummy kept them off as much as possible as they seemed to affect my breathing. I was having another bad spate of breathing. Mummy had to have another chat with the headteacher at school as my lack of attendance was severely hampering my learning. Dr Buckler was called yet again and said those familiar words: "If things get any worse today, I will come back and take her into hospital."

It was about 2am and the kettle had been boiling for several hours. Mummy was exhausted and sat bolt upright, holding me up as I struggled to breathe. Then, I became aware that something strange was happening and I started to leave my body! I looked at myself, still in my mum's arms, but I was walking away, too! How could this be? I was so broken inside as I saw the sorrow on Mummy's face, and I felt such a depth of sadness. After leaving the room, I stopped and leant against the radiator, rationalising, arguing and tried to reason with myself, looking at all the facts! Do I go back in my body? Do I choose life?

I heard Jesus clearly speak to me. He spoke with such a tender voice: "If you want to leave Earth and come and be with me, that's fine... but if you want to stay and live, you can. It is your choice. Either way, you are deeply loved!"

I agonised over the decision for some time but then I could see my body slipping away so I decided for Mummy's sake that I would return. I approached Mummy and my body really slowly as I felt slightly unsure of my decision. Life had become hard and a daily battle... but one thing was a fact: I loved Mummy and would never hurt her. And I knew that, whatever I decided, Jesus was right there with me.

....

Sunday mornings were always the same: a mixture of rushing frantically around the house to be ready to leave for church and chatter between Daddy and Mummy as to who would be preaching and how the day would unfold after being in church... twice! Mummy and Daddy always had an expectation that God would speak to them and fuel us for the following week, but I'd noticed that they were both becoming unsure about our local church as they didn't feel that it was as relevant for me and Joey anymore. We were growing up and the vast majority of other people going were growing old... I mean, really old!

Daddy was keen that we would always love being in church and that it would help us grow in our faith. So, when talk of going to the Pentecostal church a few miles away was brought up, we were both excited as they had a youth group and lots going on!

It wasn't long before we all loved the new church and started to make new friends and enjoy greater freedom in the services. I didn't miss Mrs. Hathpot's enthusiastic pumping away at the organ pedals; I had new things to do! The front row was full of girls ranging from ten-twenty years old, all playing tambourines adorned with many different-coloured ribbons. I leaned over to Mummy and, before I could say anything, she gave me an approving nod and said, "Of course you can join them." So I did!

Chapter Five
Dark Shadows

I was twelve and life felt like it was opening up a little. I loved my new church and being part of the youth group; there were two groups of girls who naturally seemed to separate themselves and I was in the group that wanted to play the tambourines and be part of anything that helped us in our journey to know God.

Cathy was the lady who very patiently taught the girls the tambourine skills; she was married and had three very small children. Nothing could have thrilled me more because I adored babies and at any opportunity would sit next to her in church and help hold the baby and play with her other little ones! She was such a kind person and we both shared a deep love for Jesus. Even though she was a good ten years older, I felt like she was my best friend and when I was at home, I didn't stop talking about her and her babies!

Mum was so pleased that I'd found a good Christian friend and that church was my favourite place to be.

"Pippa would you like to come for the day to my house? You are welcome to stay for tea, too!"

"Please, Mum! Please?"

"Okay," Mum said. "If you really don't mind, Cathy?"

It wasn't long before I started to go most Saturdays. Cathy really appreciated all the help I gave with the children and Mum was happy that I was with a lovely Christian lady! I helped feed and bathe the babies and we chatted and laughed at silly things along the way. I loved Cathy's tea because it often consisted of a homemade burger and chips! Somehow, this seemed a bit naughty as Mum would have described it as 'rubbish'. I, on the other hand, described it as 'heaven'!

Sundays came round quickly and after church one day, I was delighted to hear Mum say, "Yes: she can sleep, so long as you don't mind."

Sleep? Yay! Brill!

The following weekend, I packed my bag and arrived at Cathy's house, bursting with excitement!

Her husband, Jerry, was always around but didn't really say a lot. He was often in the chair watching TV and didn't interact a great deal with the children. I'd never really thought much about his lack of interaction with them or his dismissive attention towards me. There was no reason to, as I was fully entertained with helping out with the babies and clowning about with Cathy, dancing round the house with our tambourines!

"Pippa, if you don't mind, I need to pop out for a while," said Cathy. "I need to go to the shops. Why don't you have a bath, I will get chocolate for us and when I get back, we can have a feast!"

"Sounds perfect!" I said.

After I'd run the bath, I turned to lock the door. There was no lock! I felt a surge of panic and stood, unsure of what to do. Why isn't there a lock? Bathrooms were not my favourite places after the encounters with Uncle Ivan! After a few minutes' deliberation, I decided to get into the bath and try not to worry!

To my horror, a few minutes later, the door handle went down, and the door creaked as it opened. Jerry walked straight in then stood, bold and stern, at the side of the bath, looking down at me! I scrambled around, desperately trying to cover up.

"Lie back and carry on," he said.

My mind was in overdrive. "No! Please leave!"

He replied, "I'm going nowhere!" and sat on the toilet seat opposite the bath, looking intently at me! "Go on... wash yourself!"

I felt humiliated and scared! My heart was beating wildly, and my throat seemed to close up! He was obviously not going to move, and he stayed there until I got out! It felt like a lifetime as I couldn't move and struggled to speak.

Previous experience had told me that my feelings didn't matter and that being scared is part of life. It still didn't make it any easier when it was time to settle for the night.

Cathy and I ate the chocolate but, while she was happily chatting away, I was planning my strategy to stay safe and not let Jerry near me!

Cathy was making the bottles and finishing tidying the kitchen and said, "It's late, Pippa. You go up to bed now. Night-night and God bless!"

I crept up the stairs to bed and froze to the spot as I turned the corner near the top and Jerry was there, on the landing, masturbating! He insisted I stood to watch and up rose the familiar feeling of panic and screaming on the inside and then cutting off my feelings. Staring blankly, I waited until I had permission to move. When I was finally able to roll myself in the quilt, I cried and prayed yet again to Jesus to preserve me and get me through the night! As I was finishing praying, I gasped and took a deep breath. Jerry was coming into my room! He climbed on the bed and put his face right up to mine, his breath hot in my face. He lay there for some time and all I could do was pretend desperately, with every ounce of my being, to be asleep. Surely, he wouldn't touch me when I was asleep? Thankfully, he didn't!

Over many visits, I endured his masturbation sessions and him lying, breathing on me. My precious times with my friend were never the same again. It had escalated to the point where Jerry had put his hands in my pants, and I'd had a meltdown! My anxiety built to fever pitch as the memories of Uncle Ivan came rushing back as well as the feelings of humiliation and dread of how far this might go. Unlike Uncle Ivan's calm, calculated persona, Jerry was tense and not as gentle. My mind raced and, to add to the complexity of feelings, Jerry's little boy stood next to me, watching the whole thing. He was my little friend and I wanted to protect him, but I couldn't even protect myself!

Afterwards, I couldn't stop my teeth from chattering together; I was shaking and, once again, my legs were weak and my knees knocked together just like they did on the awful journey home from Uncle Ivan's a few years earlier. After a few incidents, I finally mustered up enough strength to say, "I'm not going to Cathy's tomorrow, Mum."

Mum said, "Of course you are! You really enjoy it there!"

"I don't want to go anymore, Mum!" Mum didn't understand. I was trapped again and didn't know what to do. I hatched a plan to slowly stop going so no one would notice why... and that's what I did. Eventually, I was free and didn't visit again! Oh, how I missed my precious friend! I was hurt and I cried myself to sleep because I felt I had hurt her, also.

············

It was the summer holidays and my new friend, Danielle from school, invited me for tea. She had a big house with lots of rooms and some which seemed like they were hidden away! I felt safe there... my friend was with me the whole time and her dad (who I'd never met) was away on business. We sang, put on a play and generally had a whale of a time. We charged Danielle's mum ten pence for the privilege of watching our carefully choreographed show!

"Pippa, your mum has called because your dad has had an accident and she says it's ok for you to stay the night."

"Is Dad ok?" I asked.

"He's just cut his arm but don't worry!"

I didn't as I was having a great time with Danielle! We put our bikinis on and sat in the bathtub for two hours laughing and making up stories. Dad's accident was the last thing on my mind, I had no idea of how serious it was and the impact it would have on him and our family.

It was Saturday as I woke up in Danielle's house and tomorrow was a big day for me: my baptism day! I'd decided that I wanted to follow Jesus for the rest of my life, and I wanted to make it a public thing. The big square pool is filled with water and the pastor dunks you under and, as you come up out of the water, it's as though you've buried your old life and your new life is just beginning! As Mum picked me up from Danielle's, I was buzzing about my baptism and, without understanding the gravity of Dad's accident, I asked her if he would be well enough to come.

"Pippa, Dad's going to be in hospital for quite a while, but you can still get baptised. Let's go and see him and chat to him about it."

I wasn't prepared for what I saw! My precious prince, my Dad, was unrecognisable! As I walked towards him, I was flabbergasted! His arms were completely bandaged with pots and surrounded by wires and drains! He had wires coming out of everywhere and he had tears rolling down his cheeks! My Daddy! I was broken-hearted. Why didn't Mum tell me how bad he was? What on earth had happened to him? I couldn't get close to him but all I wanted to do was sink into his arms! In a quiet, whispering voice, I said, "Dad, do you mind if I get baptised without you tomorrow?"

"You go ahead, Pippa. You couldn't make me more proud!"

We arrived home to see a fire engine. Mum would not let me into the garden to see, but the fire service had been called to hose it down! Dad had lost so much blood and it was over much of the garden as he had managed to walk quite a long way towards the house before collapsing and losing consciousness.

As the story unfolded, I learned that Dad had been on the roof of the greenhouse mending a broken pane of glass when the ladder slipped. He had reached forward in a split second to stop himself from falling and both arms shot through the pane of glass, completely severing his right arm and partially severing his left... all that was left was his bone! The glass had cut clean through his muscle, tendons, ligaments and arteries, his life blood had pumped out and he had been moments from death!

Joey had found him unconscious with blood pumping out of his arteries. Poor Joey!

Sunday arrived and I knew that I had made my Dad proud! I was baptised and I felt so happy and special. It was MY decision and that was so important to me as so many things in my life had been as a result of other people's decisions.

Daddy came home weeks later, unable to use his right arm and only having very limited use in his left. He didn't ever complain. In fact, he always thanked God for His goodness and I found great solace in lying my head on his chest as he talked to his Heavenly Father!

He was unable to kneel to pray at his bed anymore and I was too big to lie on his back, but nothing stopped me from lying on his chest as he gently, yet with confidence, talked and listened to Jesus. Dad taught me so much: no matter what life throws at us, we are loved and God is fighting on our behalf even when we cannot see it!

Chapter Six
Trying to Please

It was September and 'back to school'! The words I hated. But this September was more challenging than previous ones as it was time to graduate to senior school!

As the summer holidays drew to a close, the anxiety grew too. A new set of people, a new place with unfamiliar surroundings, further away from home and having to study subjects I already couldn't cope with. How I was going to grasp more information... and how would I retain it? Missing several lessons at a time was disastrous as I increasingly lost confidence in learning. It terrified me! I felt scared of being laughed at and dreaded the thought of being in trouble.

"Mum, I can't go! Please don't make me!" Mum could see how upset I was, but she was at a loss as to how to help me. Whatever she said was not the right thing! I just felt angry and alone inside. How could she know? I held so much anxiety inside and whenever another hospital admission or traumatic encounter with someone happened, I just buried it deeper down.

The eczema on my legs was improving and I didn't need the tar bandages so regularly, but I was growing up and my hormones were changing. That meant my over-reactivity to allergens was changing too! Over the summer holidays, as my legs cleared up, eczema started to spread on my face and neck. My lips and areas round my mouth were cracked and bleeding. Mum annoyed me so much as she constantly said, "Stop scratching, Pippa!" The itching was insatiable, and it would only stop once everything was bleeding. This was not a good look for my new school! Hence my old nickname resurfaced!

"Hey, Scabby! Have you infected anyone lately?"

The boys were the worst and it made me feel even more like a weirdo as I was clearly not one of the cool, good-looking girls. The feelings of inferiority and self-hate grew silently and a developing need to please everyone grew too! Mum and Dad (especially Mum) had a put a lot of importance on the fact that we *must* think how we affect the other person. "Pippa," she'd say, "God first, yourself last and others in between!" I poured all my energies into just that and so wanted to please Mum and Dad, my teachers, aunties, uncles and everyone who was in my life.

Along the way, I'd started to get the impression that the things I wanted to say or *needed* to say were not important enough and it became an everyday occurrence to let people at school laugh at me. I didn't say anything or retaliate as I knew they were right. I was ugly and I was stupid!

All this was a massive contradiction, and I knew it! Jesus was in my life, and I knew what the Bible said about me and I knew that He formed me and always had His eye on me. A deep desire to spread the acceptance and love of Jesus was increasingly becoming part of who I was, yet I couldn't reconcile all these intense negative feelings and the grief inside. "Please, Jesus! Help me, please! I cry out to you to touch my heart, I feel so alone and different from everyone else!"

The youth group was on a Friday night, and I never missed it. The leaders were cool and every week we did something different. They were always positive, and I loved being around them. The downside was that the church had an incredibly embarrassing blue bus which chugged around the surrounding villages, picking up anyone who wanted to go.

On the dot at 6.30 pm, it would come over the hill and pull up for me and my friend, Matt, to get on. Oh, we loved church! Matt was the only Christian in his house, which at times made things hard for him as they didn't understand his love for God! He was such an inspiration as he unashamedly talked about Jesus and we both got so excited discussing the things that Jesus was doing in our lives.

After school, we would meet up and hold a little meeting. It was only me and him, but we pretended there was a stadium full. I would preach my heart out one night while he then made the appeal and took up an imaginary offering and closed in prayer and then vice versa the following night. "One day, we will both preach to the multitudes!" we'd say with real conviction! Matt became my best friend and I told him everything except my darkest secrets. I knew they couldn't be told!

School had given me new challenges but ones that excited me as Matt and I were determined to tell everyone we could about the love of Jesus and what He could do for them. Over time, it became my mission to go and speak to every single teacher and staff member.

"Pippa, you can't go around saying these things!" said the rather ruffled drama teacher, Miss Bromley. However, I was determined and undeterred. The next port of call was to make an appointment with the headmaster and deputy head!

In the midst of my intense struggles and questioning about myself, nothing got in the way of my burning task to spread the *Good News*. Mr. Coatley, the Headmaster, sat with me in his office for some time. I was now twelve and felt so proud to represent Jesus. "Well, Pippa. Never lose the passion you have and thank you for sharing that with me." He spoke in a thoughtful tone, suggesting that what I said seemed to resonate within him.

....

The first two years at 'comp' had not been as bad as I had thought they would be. Another school summer holiday was approaching, and Mum was planning something with Auntie Glenda. "Pippa, how would you like to go to Uncle Ivan's and Auntie Glenda's for a couple of weeks? Your cousins, Claire and Jenny, are going too."

Oh gosh! What do I say? What do I do? I want to be with my cousins because I don't see them very often and they are so much fun... but what if Uncle Ivan hasn't changed? Surely, he's different. He's probably really sorry for what he did. All these thoughts tripped over themselves in my mind, and I couldn't think straight. I certainly couldn't show there was a problem by hesitating, so I quickly said, "Yes. That's sounds great!"

....

"Scotland here we come!" said Mum and nine hours later, we arrived!

It was a new house which helped me to feel better as old memories didn't replay but seeing Uncle Ivan's face caused a deeply troubled reaction! I tried to rationalise the situation and said to myself that I was a little girl before and he'd made a terrible mistake. He wouldn't want to make the same mistake now!

Oh, no! Why? Why did I come? Why did I ignore my fears? Why did I put everyone else's feelings above mine?

We arrived late afternoon and I soon knew that he hadn't changed at all. His eyes followed me everywhere and I knew he was just waiting for a chance! I was terrified and my anxiety caused me to go quiet and not be able to say what was wrong. I stuck very close to Claire and Jenny who laughed and messed around and, evidently, hadn't got a care in the world!

Mum had bought me a new nightie from BHS. It was a little night shirt with strawberries on it and I loved it! We were all ready for bed and sitting in the lounge and I felt really thirsty. "Please can I get a glass of water, Auntie Glenda?"

"Of course!" she said.

I went into the kitchen, and, to my horror, Uncle Ivan had followed me! He pulled me to him and started to try to kiss me! I froze solid to the spot. He got hold of my breasts and said, "It's all ok. Don't worry; I know you want this." I was completely overwhelmed and couldn't speak! Unable to react, I listened in horror as he whispered, "We have lots of time and no one will ever know!"

He let me go and I ran into the lounge, feeling like something terribly wrong was written all over me! But no! No, it wasn't! Nobody saw it! I ached for someone to see and help me... but they didn't!

That night, I lay in bed, desperate for the toilet but I didn't dare go! I realised that everyone was in bed and that someone was in the bathroom! This was my chance, I could nip downstairs and go to the loo there! Uncle Ivan wouldn't know, and I could escape his attention. I was just washing my hands quietly when a gentle knock came on the door!

Please, no! I knew it was him! What could I do? I couldn't open the door... he would hurt me! He knocked and knocked and knocked! I paced round and round the tiny room! It seemed to close in, and I couldn't breathe! My anxiety levels were through the roof!

He continued to knock. The longer I stayed in the room, the more trapped I felt but, if I were to open the door, what would he do to me? I prayed, desperately, and asked God to give me strength to open the door! I knew it was risky as he would be standing there in front of me, and anything could happen.

Eventually, I realised Uncle Ivan would not relent and I needed to get out of this prison. So, I unlocked the door with shaking hands and opened it wide with every intention of immediately running straight past him and upstairs. I wasn't prepared for what I saw. There he stood in his blue spotted pyjamas, his trousers open, and his private parts in full view! I froze again. My feet were like lead and I couldn't speak, angry at myself... so angry! I'd gone through my escape plan whilst pacing the room but, no... I was rubbish. I was a failure. I couldn't protect myself.

He stepped forward, forcing my back against the wall and, once again, I was unable to move! He started to kiss me forcefully, licking my face and hair and sticking his tongue in my ears which progressed to licking and sucking down my body. Strangely, the worst part of this event was the licking. This felt totally different from when it was just his hands as the mouth seemed to send it to another level of intimacy which repulsed and terrified me at the same time. I felt completely dirty, separated from my feelings and I was, for many years, traumatised by the memory of this event, not even able to tolerate my own husband putting his mouth near my face or neck in future years.

I found it completely unbearable and, after the tension had mounted to a point where I mentally couldn't cope any longer and things were becoming more serious, I had a surge of strength and punched the arm that had been weakened because he'd had a broken collarbone! I took my chance to squirm past him as he yelped in pain, and he smacked my behind as I made a break for the stairs. I lay in my bed, traumatised and wet through from his saliva! Rocking backwards and forwards, I sang to Jesus with tears rolling down my cheeks, sobbing uncontrollably.

The morning arrived and I hadn't slept much the night before. Once I finally stopping crying, I began to pray. I knew it wasn't God who was hurting me, and I wasn't angry at Him. But somehow, there was also a sense deep inside that the person who WAS hurting me was very lost. Although lots of my perceptions would need adjustment as I grew older, I had a heart of forgiveness from the beginning. Even though I desperately needed protection from the people who loved me, I was learning that God was protecting my heart and it would be that heart that would get me through this.

The following day, I was quite poorly with my asthma and Mum insisted I got ready for bed early. The age-old cough was as irritating as ever, and Uncle Ivan called me into his bedroom. "Here, Pippa. I've got some Lockets for you." I hesitated and thought about it. He terrified me but I just didn't have it in me not to do as I was told. It was so ingrained in me. Maybe it's ok and maybe he genuinely really does have one for me. Boy, did I need it!

He did have a packet for me and as I reached to take them off him, he started to kiss me again! I was struggling to breathe, coughing and obviously unwell, but he still took advantage of his opportunity! I quickly turned to try and get out of the bedroom, but he pulled me to him in a vice-like grip as he licked me again, put his hand up my nightie and touched my body. As I attempted to pull away, he squeezed so tight that he left marks on me. I tried so hard to get around the bed to get out, but my legs wouldn't carry me; it was as if concrete had been poured into them!

He whispered, "You see! You do want it!"

"No! No, I DON'T! Please don't!" I repeated this sentence over and over, but my voice was barely audible. The anxiety was so great that it had taken my voice away.

Where were Mum and Claire and Jenny? They were at the other end of the house watching TV. They had all been upstairs just before all this began but they had all vanished when I needed them! Uncle Ivan pushed and rubbed his body right up to me from behind. This was something he had always liked to do! I couldn't see his face, which always frightened me! I could feel everything pressing against me and I became desperate to get away! As I finally managed to shuffle towards the door, he finished what he was doing and let go of me. Running into my bedroom, I curled up under my quilt and, in my mind, I travelled far away... to a place of nothingness. I loved it there but that's where all the feelings of self-hatred and denial started setting in.

Surrounding Uncle Ivan's house were beautiful mountains and, at the end of their garden, a rippling brook which had amazing trees surrounding it and strewn across it.

"Come on, Jenny. Let's go climbing!" It was pointless asking Claire because she was the opposite of me. I was adventurous and would try anything, often climbing those trees so high that I couldn't get down without assistance! Claire just sat on the bank and waited! I found myself trying to dodge Uncle Ivan at every opportunity. Going to the stream became my solace and I climbed as high as I could till I said to myself, "No one can get me now!"

We'd had fish and chips after a lovely day walking in the mountains and as dark fell, I got ready for bed. I'd just finished cleaning my teeth and was about to run downstairs when Uncle Ivan called, "Pippa, come in here." I said that I was going downstairs but he threw me a look that I daren't disagree with and ordered, "Sit down; I've got our room ready." I felt angry and indignant! It wasn't *our* room, and I hated the fact that he'd made it sound like I agreed with him. Unable to go against his wishes, I sat down on the two-seater settee. His pyjamas were open, and he clearly had only one thing in mind. I ground my teeth and didn't know how I would get out of this one. As usual, Uncle Ivan started by saying how much I wanted this and then went on to say that this was the beginning and lots of men would do this to me. I couldn't imagine any more incidents like this! It was all too much, and I bit down hard on my lip, causing it to bleed.

He started to kiss me passionately and I allowed myself to disappear for a while, shutting off my mind. The feel of his hands on me repulsed me as, yet again, I had to succumb to the humiliation, pain and terror of being raped. But this time, it was different. He repeatedly had to force himself in me as I squirmed and managed to move enough to dislodge him. Unfortunately, this made him frustrated and even more determined which meant I had to endure the process over and over again.

During the course of the holiday, Uncle Ivan made use of every opportunity and there were new difficulties. He kissed and touched me whenever he could and was starting to treat me as if he was in a relationship with me, telling me how good we were together, while completely ignoring my feelings and what I was saying. Then he started to give me money, presumably to try and salve his conscience. I couldn't understand how he always looked happy whilst around my cousins and mum but when he orchestrated time alone with me, he looked totally different: cold, calculating and not truly interested in me or my feelings. He seemed only interested in what he could get from me to satisfy his need.

I felt broken and dirty. Who would ever believe me? I spent many hours trying to convince myself that it wasn't my fault and that eventually someone would care enough to ask how I was... and I'd dream that I could tell them!

Chapter Seven
A Broken Lifeline

After the holiday, I was finding it more difficult to want to keep 'The Secret'. I'd promised Uncle Ivan that I would never tell... and as my Dad always said, "Your word is your bond." But inside me was such confusion and conflict.

What if I dare tell someone? How would they react? But who would it be? What if I started but couldn't explain it properly or what if they didn't believe me? Maybe I could pretend I was talking about someone else... oh, but no, that would be lying! What about Matt? He'd believe me, I think. But he'd think I was so dirty! No, no! I can't tell him!

I ate another bowl of cereal. This was my fourth bowl full. I couldn't stop eating when I was stressed; I ate and ate and shovelled it into my mouth in a frenzied fashion! Somehow, being 'out of control' satisfied me, momentarily. Then I would starve myself for as long as I possibly could until Mum noticed I hadn't eaten my chocolate bars. THEN she knew that something was wrong!

"My body isn't normal," I would say to myself. "I'm ugly and stupid and weak!"

The raging topic at school amongst the girls was, 'Who did you kiss first?' They giggled and whispered and most of them were wide eyed when someone said they'd gone a little further!

I was very different! Firstly, I was a follower of Jesus and I was always open with everyone about how sex is for marriage and that's where God's blessing was. They listened intently but it often ended up being a great source of ridicule towards me. "Virgin Mary, how does it feel to be a virgin? Get used to it!"

And the boys and girls would laugh their heads off. For Jesus, I didn't mind. I believed it to be true and my love for Him extended beyond the poke of ridicule!

But something else was in turmoil. I knew I wasn't as pure as they all thought. I SO wanted to be... but it wasn't my fault! I said, "NO," so many times, I felt like a deceiver. All the giggling discussions about sex, I already understood... first-hand!

It was Friday. Yippee! That meant several things. Firstly, school was over! After I'd collected my £1.00 pocket money from Mum, I headed straight down to the corner shop for my fix of pickled onion flavoured Monster Munch, a big bag of Cola Bottles and a chocolate-covered toffee bar! Putting it in all at once, I stuck it round my teeth, spending the next hour sucking it off in sheer delight!

And the final treat (the best) was youth group! Matt couldn't come tonight as he was poorly with a sickness bug so I got on the 'blue bus' and as I travelled the 10 minute journey, I wandered away in my thoughts again.

I was a naturally happy person but the sadness inside me was growing, and it was taking on a life of its own. I found myself increasingly unable to control my emotions. I pondered over what had happened while I was at Uncle Ivan's. This particular day, everyone was chatting in the lounge and discussing when and how a person should stick up for themselves. As the conversation continued, something uncontrollable rose up in me and I sat bolt upright and almost shouted, "But what if someone is raping you?"

A stony silence had followed, and I didn't know what to do with myself! Mum had looked completely shocked and, with a look of disbelief on her face that I'd not seen before, she reprimanded me for saying such an awful and inappropriate thing. I'd felt so humiliated and left the room quietly. A few minutes later, Uncle Ivan came to find me and said, "It's all ok," while giving me a handful of money. I didn't understand. "Go on... take it; you deserve it!" he'd said. He continued to give me more after each incident, referring to it as 'payment'!

The bus pulled up to church and I went inside and sat at the back with my head down, feeling switched off in my own world. In the past, I had been able to put a front on and not show what was going off inside but after everything Uncle Ivan had just done... again... I felt tipped over the edge.

Brett, the youth leader, came and sat next to me. He was about thirty and someone I looked up to.

"Hey, Pippa. What's the matter? You're not your usual bubbly self!" I was sitting with my arms tightly wrapped around my knees, and had my head tucked tightly in. He coaxed me to look up at him. In a flurry of anguish, I blurted out, "I'm scared! Someone is hurting me!" It popped out like a cork from a bottle.

He looked puzzled and asked, "How, Pippa?"

Suddenly, all emotion left, and I felt empty again. I spoke in a monotone voice: "My uncle is touching me and making me do things I don't want to do."

As I spoke, a wave of anguish rushed through my stomach! "I've TOLD the secret!" Fear gripped me and I desperately waited for Brett's reassuring response. It didn't come! He seemed lost for words and just patted me on the shoulders, saying, "I'm sorry" and walked off to start the meeting.

Oh, I've done wrong! What a terrible thing I've just said! Brett can see how dirty I am, and he thinks I'm making it up! Maybe he doesn't believe me! I was in turmoil and felt so alone. I decided that that was it... I would never tell anyone ever again!

Brett never mentioned it again and neither did I to him.

Several weeks passed and my feelings of anger towards myself were growing. Whilst lying in bed, I would lie and punch my stomach until it was red and sore. When I could see the marks, in a strange way, it satisfied me. "Now on the outside, I can see some of the pain on the inside!" I thought to myself. I started to completely abuse the medication I was taking for my breathing problems and would take quadruple or more doses even when I didn't need it, until I was shaking and light-headed. I liked the feeling of an altered state as it felt like an escape.

Another Friday had arrived, and Matt and I were on our way to youth group on the bus. Suddenly, out of nowhere, I looked at him and said, "Can I tell you something? You are my best friend and I'm scared about something." My previous resolve to never mention it again was waning and I felt I would burst if I didn't get help! Matt looked a little worried and, raising his eyebrow, said, "What on earth are you scared of?"

Please believe me! Please! I pleaded with him not to be angry, to which he got annoyed and said, "How can I? I don't know what it's about yet!"

Ok... I took a deep breath and burst into tears. "Matt, my Uncle Ivan tried to have sex with me. He hurts me! Please, please can you help me?" At that, Matt jumped up so quickly that I jumped out of my skin! "Where are you going, Matt? Please come back!" He didn't speak a word and told the driver to stop the bus because he needed to get off. My heart felt like it had died! I loved Matt so deeply and now he hated me! It wasn't until several years later that I finally saw him again. We were both grown up and 'the conversation' was never mentioned.

I'd tried twice to get help and both times it hadn't gone well at all. Was anyone ever going believe me and help me? I decided that I had enough and would never talk about it again. I felt that it had all gone wrong because I broke my promise.

....

Uncle Ivan and Auntie Glenda often came to visit even though they lived in Scotland. Mum was always so pleased to see her sister and I had been happy to see Auntie but now that I was getting older, each visit became more challenging for me. Fortunately, after having tea with us, Uncle Ivan would go and stay at his sister's down the road but Auntie stayed with us. She talked about Uncle Ivan constantly and made strange comments - sometimes laughing about his anatomy! "Oh, your Uncle Ivan has such a big belly! Have you seen it, Pippa?" I never knew how to react!

As the years went by, I became increasingly guilt-ridden that I had this awful secret about him and the more I tried to change the subject, the more awkward things became. I loved Auntie but the pretence started to wear me down! "One day, Jesus, I need to tell her!" I said as I was praying. How that would ever be possible, I had no idea, but I knew that when I was older, it was something I had to do.

I was still fourteen and it had been a very eventful year, all for the wrong reasons but it wasn't over yet! My chest wasn't any better after several courses of antibiotics and a third course of a really high dosage of steroids. The only place for me to be was hospital. I reluctantly accepted it.

I had my strawberry nightshirt on and although it once was my favourite, I'd grown to hate it because every time I wore it, I was reminded of everything Uncle Ivan had done to me. "Mum, I need to throw this nightshirt away!" "No, Pippa. It's your favourite and it's new!"

I couldn't say that I hated it so I cut big holes in it! However, Mum just sewed them up. "Good as new!" she said. That plan failed miserably!

Now here I was wearing it in hospital. There were a thousand things going through my head, I couldn't breathe, my chest was so sore from such a series of bad infections, and I couldn't get all 'the rubbish' out of my mind.

The attack had gone on for too long, so I was given a drug that was rarely used. Another drip went up and after a few hours, my breathing started to improve. It was about 2 a.m. and I didn't feel well. My legs started jerking and before long, I was having an allergic reaction to the drug! I was in a full-blown seizure, having convulsions and then things went from bad to worse... the rare side effect of this new drug caused me to have a cardiac arrest. The ward was frantic! As I was regaining consciousness, there were several doctors around my bed messing with wires, stethoscopes and covering me up after having resuscitated me.

Eventually, they left me so I could try to get some sleep. It was then that I had another emotional outburst and couldn't stop crying... the night's events had become just too much. "Excuse me," I called to the lady in the next bed whilst still under the influence of the drugs I'd been given. "I don't know what to do. I'm scared and no one is helping me."

She sat bolt upright and said, "Tell me what you mean."

I sobbed, "My uncle keeps touching me and I don't know what to do!"

Oh my goodness! The ward came to life again! She rang her buzzer and within minutes, the nurses came. They then called the doctors who, in turn, called the police! It was like the story of the enormous turnip; one after another came to try and pull it out! I was completely overwhelmed with questions and interrogation.

Mum and Dad were called, too. It was the middle of the night, and it must have been a terrible shock when they were told, in another room, that I had disclosed some sort of abuse. Mum came to my bedside and looked so concerned. She stroked my hair and kissed me so much. Pulling up a chair, she asked me, "Who has hurt you? What did they do?" I was horrified! I never meant for this to come out, especially like this. At first, I couldn't speak, and I refused to give details of what had happened but, eventually, was able to tell her that it was Uncle Ivan who had hurt me and touched me and made me touch him. There was no way that I was going to give her more details. The drugs had worn off and, with them, my boldness had disappeared, too. I wasn't ready and I felt so scared about what would happen to me if my mum knew everything. And even worse... what would Uncle Ivan do?

The next morning, the psychologist and psychiatrist came to see me. "Hello, Pippa. I want you to tell me who hurt you." They both tried from every angle to get the information out of me, but I was too scared and locked away to be able to respond.

I never did speak to them. How could I trust them? I had no idea who I could trust. Who really cared about my story anyway?

Then, one early evening not many days after I'd been discharged from hospital, Mum shouted, "Pippa, go into your room and close the door, please. I'm making a private phone call." I immediately felt suspicious and once her and Dad had gone into the lounge and closed the door, I tiptoed down the hallway to see if I could hear what this 'too secret' phone call was all about!

"Hello, Ivan. Are you sitting down? I need you to listen and not speak." Mum sounded firm and certainly was in control of the conversation. To my horror, she went on to say, "Pippa has told us what you've done, and we believe her! We want you to know that we have made the decision to forgive you."

The phone didn't last long at all, and I shot into my bedroom and cried and cried! I felt confused and upset. How could Mum have said we know what you've done when I didn't tell her what he had done? But that was my fault... she could only guess! Over time, Mum and Dad forgiving Uncle Ivan caused mixed reactions in me. At the time, I was pleased because it covered it all over and took the attention from me, but as time and years went by, I grew to realise that what had happened was horrendous and he should have been held accountable. Nor should he have still been part of my life as I had to continue as though nothing ever happened... at a cost to my mental health.

It took six months to get well from the reaction to the drugs and the cardiac arrest and I sank into a depression.

The doctor said I'd had some sort of emotional breakdown and it would take time to be able to rebuild myself. Little did he know the extent of all the feelings I was trying to make sense of. I'd grown very attached to Dr Buckler as he'd looked after me for so many years and I so wished he'd asked me why I was so sad because I think I could have told him! But he never did.

Chapter Eight
Meeting Geoff

The long days at home were starting to pay off in terms of my drawings! I was such a perfectionist when it came to the detail and even though Mum and Dad said, "Wow, Pippa! That's good!" I would rub it out repeatedly until it was just right!

My art teacher was THE BEST and when I managed to get to school, he would sit with me during breaks and lunch times and we would draw together, challenging each other to see who could draw the most realistic face. I had another agenda, too! "So... Mr Wordsworth," I would say, in a confident, questioning tone. "Let's talk about Jesus and why we are here on this planet!" He used to laugh at me but also acknowledged that my relationship with God was more than just a handful of beliefs. We would thrash out his reasoning as to why God didn't exist and always end by agreeing that I could pray for him and 'let the best man win'! I felt I had the upper hand and rather cheekily told him so! My love for the Gospel (the good news of Jesus) kept growing and how could I keep it to myself?

....

"Pippa, I have a surprise for you!"

I ran into the back garden and my dad stood with the biggest grin on his face! My mouth dropped open! A new bike! But it wasn't my birthday! "I know," said Dad, "but I wanted to treat you! It's got a shiny new bell and I thought you'd like the basket on the front!"

"Oh, thank you, THANK YOU! I LOVE IT!"

It was sort of a metallic blue which shone with a green hue when the sun caught it. I was so happy and spent so much time riding round the village. Now I had wheels, I could venture anywhere! More pickled onion Monster Munches and pick and mix! I could be at the corner shop in exactly four minutes.

Over the years, Dad had taken Joey's bike for repairs to a local man who lived nearby. He turned his house into a bike shop, and it mystified me whenever I went in as he literally had nothing in there but bikes, chaotically piled up everywhere you looked and hanging from the ceiling. He had one filthy broken chair and a Calor gas heater in the corner. Tom, the owner, seemed a lonely old man and, to make his situation worse, he was crippled. Apparently, his mum dropped him when he was born. He wore the dirtiest overalls and smelt awful! None of that bothered me as I could see he looked sad and, of course, I knew who could help him... Jesus! So, I started to visit and talk to him. He was ridiculing and objectionable, but it didn't faze me! I thought, "Take it steady and eventually, he will see!"

Today was a teacher training day - my favourite sort of day! It was a chance to take off on my bike and see where it took me. After a visit to the corner shop for my latest fad of sherbet Dib Dabs, I rode up to Tom's. The door was open, as usual, and I shouted, "Tom! Are you there?" He came through the aisle of highly-heaped bikes, awkwardly pushed past me in his wheelchair and locked the door. I wondered why, as he'd never done that before; people wandered in and out of Tom's shop regularly, so the door was always open. Because his legs were crippled, I soon found out that his arms were incredibly strong! Pushing me into the corner, he rammed his wheelchair up to me, wedging me between it and the Calor gas heater. As I frantically looked around, I noticed he'd got porn magazines strewn across the floor and as he grabbed hold of both my arms with one hand, with the other, he started to masturbate. I felt sick and repulsed! *This can't be happening again!* I was incredibly scared... although I thought I knew him, I realised that I didn't really know him at all and had no idea of his capabilities and how much danger I was really in. "Jesus help me and get me out safely!" I prayed, desperately. Tom seemed angry and aggressive, sweat was running down his face and he had a mocking look which then turned evil. I felt that whatever was in him wanted to destroy me.

He pulled me tight to himself and the stench was awful! He dug his nails into my arms and bruised them all the way down. "Look at the pictures, look at them!" he groaned, and I felt intensely objectified and dirtied. Eventually, after he'd finished, he snapped, "Get the kitchen roll. Go on, clean me up and get down and clean the floor." Somehow, that was the hardest part. Afterwards, he laughed loudly and belittlingly.

I quickly and quietly left the shop and turned as I walked out of the door and peered round the frame and said, "No matter what, God still loves you and wants to help you and heal you!" I didn't stay for a response but peddled home as fast as I could.

On my bed that night, I sobbed and sobbed. Nowhere seemed safe and I had to swallow down the grief and somehow muster up enough strength to pretend that nothing was wrong. "Am I two people?" I asked myself. One was a nice, ordinary fourteen-year-old girl who just loved God with all her heart and the other was ugly, stupid and dirty and attracted bad men, always hiding, manipulative and lying to cover up her feelings and what had happened to her! "Jesus, forgive me. I didn't want that to happen! I'm scared and don't know what to do!"

I made sure I was well covered up so no one saw the bruises on my arms! Fortunately, I managed it but realised with alarm that I had P.E. the next day! This was already a traumatic experience for me as we were supposed to shower afterwards. I couldn't get undressed in front of anyone as I had such a fear of being naked and I felt sure that anyone seeing my body would ridicule me. Again, I lied with a crazy story to get out of another session.

By this stage, I had lost so much weight, I felt ill and had a fanatical approach to exercise. Somehow, it made me feel more in control and it was something that was my choice. I wore several jumpers to bulk me out but didn't see any of it as a problem.

To all intents and purposes, I had a lovely family that adored me, a great church family, a pastor that encouraged me and doctors who were regularly involved that I knew really well. My teachers liked me, especially my art teacher and my life was playing out in front of everyone, yet how could not one of them see I was so troubled and needed help? I really needed someone to scoop me up and keep me safe and tell me that no one was going to hurt me anymore! Oh, how I ached to be held and told I was safe!

I'd started to tell people what they wanted to hear, and I would do anything to make anyone happy. A deepening sense of failure and disappointment in myself took over and feelings of wanting to die started to play on my mind! *What if I wasn't here?* I recounted the time I left my body when I was little and questioned so often, "If I'd left Mummy and gone to heaven then all these men wouldn't have hurt me. Is it really worth hanging around?" The depression was starting again.

I wondered if everyone else cried every day. It was normal for me and when I read in the Bible that God collects your tears in a bottle, it gave me deep comfort because it meant my Jesus saw each one of them and, although I couldn't explain my feelings, I knew that He knew and loved me enough to keep hold of them.

....

It was Sunday night, and the meeting was about to start! And then... WOW! The best-looking man ever walked into church! Tall, blonde, handsome and in a smart grey suit! I was fifteen years old and that was it... I was in love! *Who is he?* There were lots of girls in church far better looking than me and definitely with better personalities. All I had was a deep love for God and a friendly smile for newcomers to the church. Oh goodness me! He was coming across to talk to me!

"Hi. I'm Geoff!"

"Oh, hi! I'm Pippa."

"It's nice to meet you," said Geoff... and that was the beginning of our chatting after every Sunday service. I couldn't believe he wanted to talk to me, but we had so much in common in our love for God that it was such easy conversation and time passed so quickly.

As time went on, we both realised that we had feelings for each other. It came as a shock to Geoff that I was fifteen when we had first started talking, but now I was sixteen nearly seventeen; Geoff was slightly older. Somehow, we didn't notice the age difference as I was quite grown up, with an old head on my shoulders. Mum and Dad were concerned and told me so, but I assured them that I was sensible and that they needn't worry. Geoff was a good man!

"Geoff, can I tell you something? You might not want to be around me after this, but I need to be honest with you."

"Of course. You can tell me anything!"

I proceeded with great caution. This was a huge risk as everyone else had left me after I'd opened up. I knew that he deeply cared about me, and I also knew that I had to take this risk! I'd learnt, that with God, we sometimes have to step out in faith and trust Him... that He will go before us and make it right.

After an honest, rather gruelling conversation, I sunk down, expecting the worst! Geoff's eyes filled with tears. He reached forward and asked if he could hug me. "Pippa, no one should have gone through all that. I believe everything you are telling me and I'm here for you." I had found someone who loved me for me and only wanted the best for me! "Together, with Jesus' help, we can sort this," Geoff said in a firm but kind voice.

Negotiating my way forward wasn't that easy, though, as my feelings felt rather mixed up. I knew I loved Geoff and wanted him to be a permanent part of my life, but I started to realise that even though I was older now it didn't cause things to vanish, and it wasn't any easier than being small. I always thought that when I was grown up, things would make sense and iron out and I wouldn't feel the same. It was soon obvious that my experiences were part of me, and I had a long journey ahead of me to try to restore the damage that these experiences had caused, and a long process would unfold with many struggles and battles along the way.

Chapter Nine
False Hope

I felt proud to be sporting a real diamond and sapphire engagement ring. I was sixteen and all I'd ever dreamt of was being married, having a little house and my very own babies - not borrowed ones! The occasional visit to school was my chance to show it off and, for once, I felt so important and grown-up and the kids who had teased me were quite shocked as they watched me climb into Geoff's shiny red Scirocco sports car at home time whilst they clambered onto the school bus.

"Pippa, he's so much older and he's more experienced than you!" Mum said with much concern in her voice.

"I know, Mum, but I love him, and he loves me!"

Mum and Dad agreed that he did seem to make me happy and said, "We don't know how long you will live," which I found very disconcerting but I was also used to hearing it.

So, they reluctantly agreed. It didn't help that my pastor at the time said, "He's too old for you, Pippa, and he will hurt you!" I accepted that everyone was only looking out for me, but my mind was set.

Geoff and I loved being in church together and spent lots of our time helping out with the youth group and taking them to other churches for youth events. We spent hours talking about Jesus, thrashing out our beliefs and challenging each other to greater things.

Communication was our strength and we discussed everything. I was rather old fashioned and decided that I needed to have everything thrashed out (even our thoughts on how we would bring up our children) before I would actually be his girlfriend. At the time, Geoff smoked, and I said with firm conviction, "It's them or me. You have one week!" I won! Things were evidently becoming a problem as I struggled to adjust my mind to a relationship. The inward battles raged as I felt confused over my security, what was acceptable and who I was. How could Geoff fancy me? He was so handsome and confident, and I was insecure and plain and wore dresses from Marks and Spencer with big bows! Mum thought they were classy and insisted on me always looking smart.

I loved the fact that Geoff was older, had his own opinions and was independent. He arrived one day and said that there were some amazing things happening at a church he had heard about. "The preacher is so passionate and it's a big church with lots of people. Let's go and see it on Sunday." I agreed and we loved it. Everyone was so welcoming, and it felt like a good move to make.

Mum and Dad were disappointed that we were leaving our local church but, as ever, they were just happy that I was pursuing my journey with God and enjoying it with Geoff. Mum and Dad had served God together through thick and thin and their reliance was certainly on the Lord, who gave them a deeper love and respect for each other.

As time passed by, Geoff was patient with me and gently and calmly talked me through so much of the difficult experiences I'd encountered. He explained that my reactions were normal. I hadn't felt safe, so it was natural that when put and in new situations or challenging ones, I reverted back to patterns of thinking that made sense to me at the time. I was upset with myself as my memories were still fresh at times and Geoff's kisses or closeness were triggers to those traumatic feelings and memories. I felt like I had let God down and, although in lots of ways I was becoming stronger in my faith and more Christlike in my character, I couldn't shake off the deep things locked away that still made no sense to me, no matter how I tried to tackle them.

It wasn't long after joining the new church that, after lots of discussion, we decided it might be helpful to talk to them about my childhood experiences. They happily agreed and, after a lot of encouragement, Geoff took me to see them. I was incredibly tense and worried to death that they would tell me off because, somehow, I felt that everything was always my fault. But on the other hand, perhaps in a naive way, I completely assumed somebody could definitely help me.

We were very surprised that they said we should arrive at 11.00pm and thought that was incredibly late and unusual. I was immediately put out as I thought I would be talking to the pastor and maybe his wife but, to my shock and horror, there was a room full of people. The pastor, his wife, two elders, the assistant pastor and his wife, another onlooker who I had never seen before... and us!

I was only sixteen and my confidence was in my boots at the best of times so this was gruelling. They began, one by one, to ask intrusive questions and delve into what turned out to feel like an interrogation and the longer it went on, the more shame I felt. We left completely bemused and shocked by what had just happened. The main content of the conversation was how sex outside of marriage is wrong and it is of upmost importance to keep our minds pure! I completely agreed with their stance on relationships, but I had dared to open myself up. I had shared my most painful experiences and gone against the promise I made to Uncle Ivan... and their response devastated me. Rather than love me through this and actually try to help me through something that wasn't my fault, they heaped more guilt and shame on an already-heavy heart.

Together, we tried to rationalise this over the next few weeks and, as ever, Geoff was on my side. We agreed that they had made a terrible mistake and made a poor judgement and that this wasn't my fault. I chose to forgive their complete ignorance and tried to put it behind me.

Several weeks later, I was asked to stay back and speak with an elder after church. I sat down next to him and was intrigued as to what he might want to talk about.

"I know you were only very young when you were abused but you need to take responsibility and accept that it was your fault. When you were little, you wanted sex." Elder Terry said it in a calm, cold manner, staring into my eyes without blinking. I nearly fell off the chair! I was on my own and had no one to stick up for me and defend me.

Deeply wounded, I tried to fight back my tears, saying, "That may be what you think, but you are VERY wrong!"

"Well, that's the way I see it!" was all the response I got.

I had no strength to challenge him and even less confidence, so I stood up and left quietly. I couldn't tell Geoff what he said as I felt so ashamed and confused by what had happened. My trust had been shattered again. I had dared to believe that I could get help but, yet again, it had been false hope!

I felt that I must be an evil person and that no one trusted me. This made me start to believe that maybe it WAS my fault. That maybe that was why it had happened so much. I was deeply unhappy and felt trapped from every angle. The place that I had sought healing and help was quickly proving to offer quite the opposite.

Sundays were such busy days, but we were used to that; after all, I'd gone to church twice on a Sunday all my life! Our new church was quite a distance away, so people were very kind and often invited us back for Sunday lunch and to stay until the evening service. Peter (another one of the elders) and his wife started to regularly invite us. They cooked a lovely Sunday roast which was very welcome as some of the meals other people cooked were made with love but tasted awful. We would smile and gulp them down very gratefully, regardless!

After lunch at Peter's, we'd take it in turns to wash up while everyone else sat down, chatted about the morning service and generally relaxed with their feet up. Peter always asked me to help him do the pots.

On this particular Sunday afternoon, I was busy drying the plates and Peter called me over. He had perched on a stool, and as I turned to face him he quickly lifted me up off the floor and pulled me close and dragged me down his body. He had an erection and slowly forced me to rub over it. Horrified, I looked up and found that, yet again, I couldn't speak. I felt the old familiar choking feeling in my throat and my heart started to pound out of my chest! *Why is Peter doing this? He's an Elder and a husband and a father!* He repeated the same repulsive action and made sure I felt his erection again. Fortunately, he changed his position, so I quickly took the opportunity and ran into the lounge. Geoff could see something was wrong and whispered, "What's the matter? Why are you upset?"

"I can't tell you right now. I will later."

Geoff was angry and in disbelief when I told him. I pleaded and begged him not to say anything. I couldn't cope with a confrontation and the humiliation that it would put me through! I already had enough shame going on so Geoff agreed to stay quiet. Unfortunately, Peter and his wife invited us around the most and it was a very awkward situation. I desperately wanted to normalise what had happened and to give him the benefit of the doubt and I managed to convince Geoff that this was the best thing to do. After all, they were Elders in the church, and we had always been taught to put ourselves under their authority no matter what.

Geoff didn't take his eyes off me during those long Sundays, and I was very thankful! Peter didn't repeat his actions but made more inappropriate suggestions when he thought he could get away with it.

Then one day, after we had been talking about summer holidays and swimwear, he came into the room with one of his daughter's bikinis and said, "Come on, Pippa. Put this on and show us how good a bikini can look!"

I went bright red and quickly snapped, saying, "No way! I don't want to!" I was angry and felt even more upset that he was supposed to be an Elder in the church. His actions were far from Christlike. Geoff sort of laughed it off and tried to smooth over a very awkward silence while Peter acted as though he'd done nothing wrong and was just complimenting me! It was far from a compliment as far as I was concerned. I felt dirty and cheap. He was in his late forties, and I was only sixteen.

We never went there again for our Sunday dinner, but he continued to act inappropriately at church and joined the clan of men who did it under the radar of other people's attention while no one noticed (or chose not to acknowledge it). After what the leadership had said and how they obviously felt about my past, there was absolutely no way I felt I could tell anybody. I didn't talk to Geoff about it as I felt that enough had happened... and conflict was something I avoided at all costs!

Years later, it came to light how overly controlling this church had been with its members certainly being nowhere near a healthy representation of the Lord's church. The church was closed down and there have been several suicides by members. Many people had lost their homes and marriages had broken up. By the grace of God, we had managed to get out, relatively intact!

Chapter Ten
Changing Seasons

My eighteenth birthday had come and gone but that had no significance to me as all my attention was on my wedding day in six weeks' time. I was bursting with excitement and was enjoying every bit of the planning.

Geoff was happy to let me make most of the decisions and the preparations went without a hitch. We had trawled round Liverpool to find the perfect wedding dress material. Fortunately for me, my soon-to-be Mother-in-Law was a dress maker! Dad came with us, and we kept losing him as he continually wandered off without thinking. He was my only concern... he was my world, but I was losing him as his Alzheimer's had taken another dip.

The Big Day arrived, and Mum wore a beautiful dress and hat but made a last-minute decision to wear a long string of pearls over the top! Not a good look as she looked like the Mayoress! We only noticed this weeks later when looking back at the wedding photos! I couldn't stop laughing and, after she'd got over her annoyance of how she looked, she found the funny side, too.

Dad got himself into a pickle over what he had to say once he'd walked me down the aisle! "I do! That's all, Dad!" I repeated it over and over, but it didn't lodge and as we walked together arm in arm down the aisle, I whispered in his ear, "I DO!" Moments later, he'd forgotten it, but it was a minor hiccup, and it became something I would remember with such fondness and humour. He, on the other hand, was immensely relieved when his moment was over, and I don't think **he** found it funny!

As Geoff and I stood as man and wife greeting all our guests into the reception hall, I'd completely overlooked the fact that Uncle Ivan would greet us too! He kissed me on both cheeks and squeezed me, making my stomach turned over. I was increasingly struggling to be around him and even the mention of his name caused a reaction in me but, as ever, I kept it to myself. If only I had mustered the strength not to invite him and if only Mum and Dad's forgiveness hadn't overshadowed wisdom (which, I think, would have been to keep him away from me and out of my life). Fortunately, he stayed well away from me during my special day.

The next couple of weeks were a shock to my system as I found myself in France on honeymoon with what felt like a strange man, away from home and my mum and dad, who were my security. My attachment to my mum wasn't normal but I was unaware at the time. Up until getting married, I'd want to be near her or have her in sight or available at any time and when she was at work, I felt bereft and longed for her to come home. I couldn't eat when Mum was out as the anxiety in the pit of my stomach felt like it prevented me from doing so. My attachment to Dad was a mixture of complex feelings as I loved him deeply and constantly told him so. However, I had a fear that one morning I would wake, and he would be dead. He was now in his seventies, and he felt so old to me. I tried to put right the years when I was scared of him tenderly tucking me into bed. As a little girl, I had cried myself to sleep night after night - wanting him near but confused about my feelings. Wanting to be held so tight but scared to be. I loved him so much! What would I do if he died? The fear of not having Mum and Dad near was, at times, debilitating. Marriage made me feel like I had lost them!

Geoff was incredibly kind, but I could tell that he wondered what on earth had hit him: he had all this emotion to deal with!

To add insult to injury, my breathing problems were bad, and Geoff had to take me to hospital, using £70 of our tiny budget to pay for a lifesaving injection. Fortunately, we found a little tavern that gave us two plates for one meal and a free glass of vino each. I was now married yet felt incredibly guilty as I knew that if Mum and Dad could see me, they would be so disappointed in me! Indulging in 'demon drink'! Hardly the romantic holiday we'd both planned for so long but, nonetheless, we survived it and much to my relief, we eventually returned home and began a new life together.

This was the first of many holidays abroad but rather than the logic of 'the more you do it, the easier it will become', the opposite was true. I had a gut-wrenching feeling whenever I went away or ventured into unfamiliar settings. My distrust of men and fear of what they were thinking and how safe I was just steadily continued to grow. As my friends talked about what they wanted to achieve and discussed their bucket list, I realised that I had no desire to go anywhere and my ambition for my life was to stay within the walls of my home.

It wasn't my age that let me down as I felt ready for my own little home and my independence. I kept home well and enjoyed being married but it was my inability to reign in my insecurities and fears that was growing. In some ways, I'd been forced to grow up quickly as I'd had to build a resilience and strength to get me through illness and trauma and, as a result, was more mature than my peers – but, in other ways, the damaged little girl was stuck in her infancy and there grew a void between the younger and the older me.

The older me loved people and enjoyed helping out in the church and I found myself walking in Mum's footsteps with design, decorating, papering and transforming my house into a home. I loved being a wife and found myself supporting Mum. She was now struggling to care for Dad, who had lost all sense of reality.

On the other hand, the little girl in me had never been listened to or helped, so her inward battles were so deep and entrenched that she knocked the grown-up me off-balance when faced with a trigger. This was anything that caused me to remember or feel the traumas I had gone through as a child and young person. To any onlooker or even a family member, I didn't show any outward sign of struggling. I became very proud of myself for being able to put on such a good show. I saw this as a strength and was determined not to let this struggling part of me have a life. God was my life and I wanted, more than anything, to represent him well.

I knew from reading the Bible and from my relationship with God that He looks into and reveals the secrets of the heart, which leads Him to help His children to reach for Him and be free. But, no matter how I tried to shake off how I inwardly felt and no matter how I tried to change the 'hidden' me, I couldn't! I went round in a continual cycle of disillusionment and a deep sense of anger towards myself.

The longer this went on, the stronger it became, and I continually pushed down all my feelings and tried to cut off from them. Feelings of being disconnected and denial were welcome as I began to believe that what had happened in the past wasn't a big deal and actually Uncle Ivan wasn't so bad. On the news were such horrific things and paedophilia seemed to be more prevalent. Years were passing by without any acknowledgement of the past and Uncle Ivan and Auntie Glenda were treated as welcome as anyone to Mum and Dad's. I adopted the attitude that pleasing everyone was my mission and I wanted everyone around me to be happy. If I delved into my past, then no one was a winner!

Geoff and I were now our own family unit, but new tensions were growing as Auntie Glenda wanted to stay with us in our new home when she came down to visit her family. Geoff and Auntie had a strained relationship. I think Geoff struggled with what he knew and didn't like how much she talked about her husband. She occasionally ventured into saying inappropriate, intimate things about their relationship or his body parts. "Why is she saying this stuff?" Geoff would say. I was confused as I absolutely had no idea how much she knew about what Uncle had done to me, or if she knew anything.

Instead of me siding with him, I found myself trying to defend her. I think I was trying to disarm the situation and smooth things over. I automatically assumed that Geoff was ok but could see that Auntie was fragile and emotional. The years ahead were a very difficult journey watching Auntie Glenda go through a mental breakdown, paranoia and an obvious desperation to be liked. She would be over-familiar with all the male members of my family. None of them reciprocated but it left me in the middle, trying to hold it all together. Mum had drilled into me how hard her sister's life had been and that it was our job to be kind and tolerant. After all, we were the Christians, and her need was greater. Auntie Glenda was becoming as hard to handle as Uncle Ivan. I was facing a completely different set of complex and costly challenges, which lasted many years.

Chapter Eleven
A Nest Full of Chicks

We had been married for three years and we were on our third house. Geoff knew how to spot a property that he could do up for us to sell for a profit. I was the interior designer and, in-between hospital admissions one week out of every four, we managed to do them up and start looking for the next one.

Geoff meant the world to me but within our relationship there were difficulties. These stemmed back to both my early childhood and Geoff's as he had not had the best rôle models for parents. I was insecure and he was angry at times. Not a great combination but one that we both knew God could sort out if we kept seeking Him and kept putting Him first in our relationship.

The physical side of our marriage was often under strain. Irrespective of how I tried, I could not erase the memories and the feelings in my body that were put there by Uncle Ivan. Regularly crying after we'd been intimate, I felt guilty and dirty more often than not. I couldn't have articulated the feeling as a child and young person but now I was older, my feelings of objectification felt part of me.

Mum was, in no uncertain terms, clear about what I should and should not be wearing. "Pippa, your top is too low!"

On the other hand, Geoff was saying, "Pippa your mum has no right saying what you should wear! Your top is too high; I like it lower!"

Mum wanted me in her Marks and Spencer's dresses and Geoff wanted me in a miniskirt. I was so tired of trying to please everyone. Uncle Ivan had damaged my confidence and my ability to stick up for myself but, in actual fact, I had no idea what was right and what was wrong. Being in hospital so much had left me feeling like a number, *the men* had made me feel like an object, Geoff made me feel 'not enough' and Mum's catchphrase was, "And you are supposed to be a Christian?"

As a young lady, I felt plain, and Mum said I was manly. I wasn't allowed make-up and I certainly couldn't have ever looked slightly sexy or attractive as a woman. My self-image was in tatters as I didn't want to look cheap or ungodly, but I would have liked to feel pretty and attractive. Inside, I felt angry because she said I looked manly... but who was making me take on that image?

Geoff always said I was beautiful, and I knew he meant it. He wanted to show me off and said, "If only you had confidence, Pippa!" Geoff didn't want to be pushy and had tried his hardest to be patient, but he got frustrated and angry at times as there never seemed to be any improvement despite me trying to be what he wanted me to be.

One Sunday, we'd had a visiting preacher from Keith Green ministries who shared her testimony of how she'd gone through sexual abuse and how God had set her free from all the complexities of it. I felt my face colour up and I felt as though I'd got a beacon flashing on my head that said, "Me too," much to my horror! I squirmed and felt awfully uncomfortable but couldn't help but question inside myself whether I could ever be given the same time, space and opportunity to be honest about my abuse. I was looking at the book stand at the back of church after the meeting, and I noticed a leaflet entitled *How to Survive and Heal from Sexual Abuse*.

My heart started to pound, and I coloured up again. Dare I pick it up? Quickly, while no one was looking, I grabbed one and shoved it into my pocket. This was the first thing that truly started to hit the nail on the head for me. It made sense and I identified with everything written in it. I read it, re-read it and devoured it until I almost knew it off by heart. One thing was for sure: what had happened to me wasn't right and all the negative feelings and fears I had were described as **normal** in the leaflet. The relief I felt when I read it was overwhelming.

Even so, I kept it well-hidden - especially from Geoff - as I felt embarrassed. I would get it out, repeatedly, when life felt really tough and my mind was playing tricks on me. At that time, it was like a healing balm that soothed me. I was so grateful to the Lord for leading me to it.

Just before my 21st birthday, I gave birth to my first beautiful child. As all the other mothers slept on the ward, I held my newborn daughter in my arms and prayed over her all night. I cried out to the Lord that she would know him and experience the same love that I had experienced from an early age. The unconditional love of God. I knew she was given to me to nurture and protect, and I cried so earnestly that she would be protected from sexual abuse. I dedicated her to God the first night after her birth. With every ounce of my being, I prayed blessing over her and consecrated her to work for him and fulfil the plans that the Lord had for her. We couldn't believe how blessed we were. Geoff was in love all over again!

It was a hard year as my breathing had been particularly bad due to high pollen counts so I'd had ten hospital admissions. But good news came as I found out I was pregnant again. We'd just had homemade chips and fried egg! One of our favourites but also a good opportunity to save a bit of money - usually to buy more skirting boards or plaster. After putting Joy to bed, we looked at the pregnancy stick and two lines appeared! Yippee! Another precious baby! I was ecstatic!

Several weeks later, I noticed that I was bleeding and the sonographer said, "I'm sorry to have to tell you but your baby is barely attached. It may attach or it is more likely that it will come away. I'm very doubtful you will keep this baby." Sure enough, the next day, I'd lost the baby. We were sad and disappointed, but I had an overwhelming peace and understanding that nature has a way of selection and I was blessed with baby Joy. God was in control, and I rested in Him.

Dad was in a bad place now as his Alzheimer's had taken all his personality. I was twenty-three and I missed him so much. He'd not been my Dad, in his ways, for seven years. Mum was struggling to care for him as he couldn't stand up and when she got him up, he couldn't sit down. Although a lot of what Dad did was very sad to watch, his little walking sprees were hilarious. I caught him, on several occasions, pushing his stick upside down along the pavement. It looked like he was looking for some treasure with a metal detector! I couldn't stop laughing! Mum thought it was funny but couldn't get him back inside quickly enough, checking all around that the neighbours hadn't seen! He didn't know who any of us were and we were devastated but accepted that he needed professional care. So, reluctantly and with a broken heart, we succumbed, and he went into a home.

Only a week later, he was rushed to hospital dehydrated and in a real state. My precious Dad! My heart was wrenched to see the pathetic state in which he'd ended up. Three weeks later, he was found on the floor, his hip broken... and he was broken, too. As he lay in his hospital bed, I cried out to the Lord to take him home. Heaven was where he belonged now. His mind and body had finished their race. He had accomplished what he had set out to do. He'd taught me and Joey how to find God and he'd lived a life that underpinned everything he professed. I visited every day and washed him and kissed him and kissed him again. "My Prince, I love you!"

We called Joey, who rushed to the hospital as quick as he could. Geoff prayed, "Lord, thank you for Dad and we release him to you!" I felt his pulse weaken beneath my fingers as it slowly stopped beating. A tear rolled down his cheek and he was gone. Oh, Daddy!

I uncovered his terribly-injured arm and said, in a final, angry tone, "That's it! You can't hurt him anymore!" I snipped off a chunk of his soft shiny grey hair (from underneath, of course) to keep and remember him. He looked peaceful and all the years of silent pain with his arm and all his own personal struggles with social anxiety were finally over! Why had I anguished over losing him during my whole childhood? After getting through the initial shock and loss, I realised the fear that I'd carried had been such a waste of emotion. I felt blessed that, although I wasn't that old, I was grown up and he had given me all I needed to get through life and that I could survive without him.

After difficulty in getting pregnant, I was ecstatic to find out that, sure enough, I was eight weeks pregnant. By twelve weeks, I recognised the same feelings that I'd experienced during the last pregnancy: an increasing lack of symptoms. Surely this couldn't happen again, could it? Twenty-four hours later, I'd had the remnants of another baby surgically removed.

"Lord, something is not right!" I talked it through with Him and again found a level of peace. I was sad but hadn't lost hope that one day, I would hold another baby in my arms.

That October 31st, I will never forget! Geoff and I had just gone to bed, and we were chatting about the two babies we had lost. We both came to the conclusion God only wanted to bless us and we both felt that He wanted this next baby here safe and sound. Geoff put his hands on my stomach and, immediately, something strange started to happen. It felt like something awful was punching me on the inside and my body jumped and kept leaving the bed as if whatever was inside me wasn't happy that its position was challenged. Geoff said, "Barrenness! I command you to leave! You have no place here!" At that, my stomach lurched with a last almighty thump, I felt something leave. It was a spirit of barrenness, seeking to destroy God's blessings. That night, I conceived our son.

Before he was born, a lady said to me, "May I tell you something the Lord has just told me?" You are going to have a son and you will see him sooner than expected. He is special and God has chosen him to bring healing and call many people back to His God." Geoff and I were humbled and delighted as it was our deepest desire that our children fulfilled the reason they had been given life: to know God intimately, above anything else.

Sure enough, he was a boy, and he came five weeks early. Lewis arrived perfect and beautiful! The rest of the prophecy was to unfold in years to come.

On the one hand, our life was good: we had a girl and a boy, and I felt incredibly blessed - they were healthy, and, to onlookers, things looked peachy. However, it wasn't long after Lewis was born that I struggled with a heavy cloud of depression. I could only describe it as like a little person constantly crying inside me, repeating over and over again, "Please help me!" I cried most days, and this went on for ten years. I couldn't find anyone to help me deal with the root of my deep sense of sadness inside. Geoff's uncle was a missionary to Africa, and he was very close to Geoff. Through the course of conversation, he picked up that I needed help. We agreed to meet for four weeks for an hour. It turned out to be rather a painful process as he was following a written paper which guided a minster through abuse! Some of it wasn't relevant and he looked shocked at some of my basic revelations. I certainly couldn't tell him everything as he'd have died on the spot! It was embarrassing and like pulling teeth. I was so glad when we called it a day. But, yet again, I was left deeply disappointed that I'd barely scratched the surface and I so desperately wanted to be free.

Breastfeeding was difficult as I was totally attached to my beautiful Lewis, but the sensation reminded me of Uncle Ivan. It triggered awful sensations and, somehow, I felt so alone. Although my son was a male, I am so pleased that my negative experiences didn't put a distance between us. He was my pride and joy and I'm deeply grateful to God that my distrust of men didn't at all affect my relationship with my Lewis.

Not long after he was born, I fell pregnant again! It was a shock to us both and we didn't feel ready for another baby! But I believed that children were a beautiful blessing, so it wasn't long before we were starting to plan for another arrival. We held hands and waited with anticipation as the sonographer switched on the machine. I was three months pregnant, or so I thought. Oh no! I had seen that face before and Geoff saw it, too. We looked at each other and then heard the words, "I'm so sorry but there's no baby in there." The sac, cord and everything was growing but a baby wasn't developing! We were both silent and just listened to the nurse making arrangements for *another* operation later that day.

I recovered quickly and got on with life. We were moving to Bedfordshire to join a new church and excitedly packed the van, saying goodbye to a house that had seen so many joys but also many hard times too. Joy and Lewis were with Mum for the day and I'd had a sneaky suspicion that I could be pregnant again! The test was positive and as we chugged along in the removal van, I turned to Geoff and said, "New house, new baby!" Eight months later, our precious Bella was born! She arrived on Lewis' second Birthday! What a perfect present she was! Lewis, on the other hand, wasn't impressed. Being two, he was far more interested in his shiny new tractor and a great big piece of his own birthday cake!

Six pregnancies later, I'd managed to keep three and three was the final number. Geoff said, "That's it!" and boy, did I agree!

....

A year later, we were faced with a huge challenge of faith which began with Lewis often falling over when he was running around, and his legs appearing to keep giving way. We had begun to notice that he cried in the evenings and rubbed his legs, which was accompanied by a groaning sound. It wasn't long before we decided to take him to the doctor to get this mystery checked out. To our horror and disbelief, Lewis was diagnosed with a sarcoma (a form of cancer) which presented as a malignant tumour on his growth plate in his knee.

He was such a handsome little boy with white-blonde hair, big blue eyes and dimples in his cheeks. It was Easter and he was three years old. We remembered what the lady had said to us in church that evening when I was pregnant with him: "This boy will become a man who leads many people back to the Lord, his God!" What a promise! The Lord had spoken to me about his future as well, so this trial came as a shock! We believed in the power of prayer, and I remembered what my Dad had taught me, from when I was a little girl, that our God's name is Jehovah Rapha: our God that heals.

The process moved very quickly from Lewis going to see the GP right through all the different scans, blood tests and examinations and finally being admitted to Birmingham Cancer Hospital. It took just seven weeks and happened like a whirlwind!

The children's cancer ward was incredibly sad. There were so many critically ill children: lots with missing limbs, no hair, or frameworks around body parts that had been partially removed. The walls around the ward had posters plastered everywhere about bereavement and dealing with the death of a child. We couldn't believe our special little Lewis was tucked up in bed alongside all these other children. We had left grandparents, family and friends back home distraught at the thought of losing him.

We didn't know how this was going to work out and, as a mum, I felt helpless, but we knew God was so near. Churches all around the world were praying and we couldn't give up hope as that's part of the nature of the God we serve.

"Geoff, what are we going to do if he dies?" We fell into each other's arms sobbing as we tried to come to terms with what was happening. Lewis was asleep and the Consultant took us into another room.

"Mr. and Mrs. Rafael, Lewis is very sick, and we need to discuss amputation of his leg if we are to have a chance to save him. We also need to check his chest for secondary growths. We are not hopeful."

Our world, at that moment, felt like it collapsed. Eventually, we gathered ourselves together and both went in separate directions to have space to pray and refocus. The consultant came to find us to tell us that first thing in the morning they were going to give him his final scan CT scan to evaluate whether the amputation was viable.

That night, we called everyone we could and asked them to pray in faith. We knelt at the side of Lewis's bed, and we prayed, "Lord, we love you and we thank you for giving us our beautiful little boy. If we were only meant to have him for three years, then we accept that, and you can take him. We love you, Father, and we trust you with our son. We give him to you and have your way, Lord. No matter what happens we love you!"

The morning arrived and our little boy lay there in the tube. He was so brave and was told he must not move at all. Not an easy task for a three-year-old, but I kept plying him with polo mints and he was doing great! As the imaging was being done, Geoff and I spoke in tongues the whole time until, suddenly, there was a huge bang and the CT scanner and the computers (in fact, all the computers in the hospital) went down! It took the rest of the day to reboot them.

Lewis finally had his scan in the evening. The results were back, and the consultant came with a crowd of other doctors, too, saying, "Mrs Rafael, please walk with Lewis to the end of the ward and back." As we returned, he said, "Well, we can't explain it at all, but you have a perfectly healthy son!"

His repeated scan showed no tumour at all - just a fine pin-prick mark on the bone. "We can't explain it, but he will need to be repeatedly scanned for a year. Other than that, you can go home."

God had given us a miracle! Our son would grow up to fulfil the plans God had told us about before he was born. We drove home stunned, exhausted and so deeply grateful to God!

Chapter Twelve
Never-Ending Cycles

The children were growing up and the household had seen so many changes. Much to the kids' delight, we had had rabbits, mice, too many guinea pigs to count, chickens which had their nails painted regularly, and turkeys to whom we gave a marvellous life and in return, they gave their life for us at Christmas. That's what I told the kids and they accepted it quite happily.

Although the children were doing great, Geoff and I were struggling. We loved each other so much but I felt so low and often felt disconnected to him. I felt like I was in my own world and no matter how much I prayed and pleaded with God to set me free, I didn't really know what I needed freedom from. I felt confused and alone.

It was then that I made one of my biggest decisions up to that point... and that was to tell Auntie Glenda what Uncle Ivan had done all those years ago. Occasionally, she was still coming and staying with us, and I felt a fraud because I carried a heavy weight when she was around as I felt that I had betrayed her. Even though I wasn't a willing participant in Uncle Ivan's horrid games, so many years of relationship with Auntie had gone by and I'd acted like nothing was wrong and I'd had to put up with all the stuff she said about him. Enough was enough and I had to speak out. So, I crafted a plan! Geoff was in agreement. He got the children to bed and went out.

Auntie had been visiting Mum for the day and was due back home for sausage casserole at 7.00 p.m. The scene was set, and goodness knows how I was going to eat knowing what I was about to launch into afterwards!

Cups of tea in hand, we sat down on the sofa. "Auntie, I want to talk to you. Erm, I need to tell you something." A long pause ensued.

"Pippa, you're scaring me!" snapped Auntie Glenda. "What on earth are you trying to say?"

"Well, it's so difficult for me to say this but..." Another long silence. I had my usual choking feeling and my throat felt like it was closing up. My stomach threatened to bring up the entire contents of my forced-down casserole!

"What's happened?" Auntie was starting to go red with nerves and it was travelling up her neck. She was agitated and impatient. "Pippa, are you getting divorced?"

"No! It's not that..." From the depths of my heart, I cried out to God for help, took a huge breath and said, "When I was little, Uncle Ivan hurt me."

Auntie's eyes opened wide, and she snapped, "What do you mean?"

"He touched me and made me touch him!"

"WHAT? What did he do?"

I was flabbergasted as I'd expected her to absolutely deny that he was capable of such a thing. "I can't go into detail, Auntie!" I was out of my depth and had no idea how this was going to pan out. She pressed for more details, but anxiety overwhelmed me, and I completely began to clam up. There was no way I could tell her everything. I hadn't managed to get top side of all the consequences of his actions so there was no way I was going to make myself vulnerable to her, too.

She asked when it had happened and then she said the one set of words I never expected to hear but so needed: "I believe you, Pippa."

By this time, she was in a real emotional state; she was shaking, and her full neck and face were lobster-red. I felt so sorry for her and heartbroken that I had caused her so much pain due to this awful revelation.

To my horror, she suddenly scrambled to get her handbag and desperately fumbled inside for something. Grabbing her phone, she began to make a call. I shot forward and, in a terrified voice, spluttered, "Auntie! What are you doing? Who are you calling?"

She didn't answer me! She was in her own desperate world and, as tears rolled down her cheeks, the recipient answered the call.

"Sarah! Sarah!" Auntie had called my cousin (her daughter), who could have never envisaged such a call that evening! "Pippa has just told me your Dad has touched her! Has he touched you?"

I wanted to crawl under the settee! It was all too much. I sat and listened to the emotionally charged, desperate phone call. To my relief, Auntie Glenda came off the phone quite quickly. She gave out a huge sigh of relief and said, "At least he hadn't touched my Sarah!"

Auntie continued to press for more information. "Why won't you tell me what he did?" I was utterly embarrassed and ashamed and needed to end this dreadful evening so, as best as I could, I told Auntie the bare minimum to save her feelings and to try to maintain my dignity, too. "Auntie you know how precious you are to me and how sorry I am that I've caused such upset, but I had no choice but to tell you this. I've held it in for so long!"

Auntie Glenda left with a heavy heart, and I felt responsible... but she never asked how I was! At the time, that didn't matter to me; all I could think about was that I'd hurt her. It wasn't until years later that I realised I wasn't her priority. Her own needs always came first and whatever happened, she always defaulted to how everything affected her.

I was shocked to hear her say, a few days later, that she had confronted Uncle Ivan and he immediately admitted that he'd hurt me. He had said, "I've done everything to Pippa that she said I've done and more." At least I was believed, and he owned up but that was where it ended. Not another word was said about the subject.

Mum and Dad had, in no uncertain terms, brought me up to abhor the 'demon drink.' The conviction my mum and dad had was not one I now shared. Geoff drank and for a long time I sat by his side with a can of Dr Pepper wanting to follow Mum and Dad's way, but now I found myself drinking red wine. Boy, did it alter things! I thought it helped because I would relax and, for a short while, not have such angst inside. Although I didn't drink copious amounts at one time, I found it hard when I 'needed' a drink but couldn't have one! This flagged up a problem that I could see but my pain was too big. I began to feel dependant on alcohol which added to my already-battered feelings of failure. "Oh, Jesus! I'm so sorry! Please forgive me and set me free!"

Even though I was in a dark place emotionally, I clung to Jesus because I knew that He was the only one in whom I could fully trust. I knew He was incapable of letting me down but boy, did I let Him down!

The weekly visits to the doctor were tiresome but part of my routine to manage my breathing difficulties. He knew me so well as I'd been seeing him for several years since I moved to Bedfordshire. He had the same concern for me as Dr Buckler, so I felt fortunate.

It was a Monday morning and I arrived at the surgery, not with any intention other than to have my breathing monitored, but, without warning, I blurted out, "Dr Stanley, can I tell you something?" I burst into tears and could not stop all the things I'd kept tightly under wraps from coming out of my mouth. I told him about Uncle Ivan, about my depression and how I felt about myself. Tears filled his eyes and we sat for an hour talking through things. He didn't seem to care about his other patients waiting and I reminded him how long we'd been; I didn't want a vigilante group accosting me as I slipped out, having taken up six appointment slots! So, I returned the next day, as he insisted on me going back, and I finally relented and accepted the antidepressant he prescribed.

Oh, how I cried when I got home! I'd let God down and myself. "Jesus is the Prince of Peace and the Wonderful Counsellor," I said to Geoff. "He lives in me, yet I feel so low!" I'd started to feel like life wasn't worth living. I knew that, as Christians, we have to be careful what we say because 'life and death are in the power of the tongue', but I often would sit in front of my mirror as I put my make-up on and look at myself in sheer disdain, saying under my breath, "I wish I was dead!"

A clear cycle was emerging that added to the root of fear of failure and of disappointment. I could see myself slipping, unable to overcome all the feelings, which made me feel distanced from God. This broke my heart as He was my 'first love' and He was the one who was trustworthy and had always been there, but I felt so ashamed and angry at my inability to conquer such negative feelings. So, up went my walls, down went another glass of wine and the demons inside were very happy.

Eventually, I would manage to negotiate and align myself to receive the grace of God that had never run out... again! And, for a while, I did well, then slowly found myself spiralling down the same track again and around it I would go, completing the cycle once more.

Where was my conviction? Who do I think I am? I hated the thought of being a hypocrite and sang over and over again, "Create in me a clean heart, oh Lord, and renew a right spirit within me!"

My children, although much older, still relied on my guidance and godly wisdom, my church appreciated my input as I was involved in prayer ministry and yet I was crumbling inside! The guilt and condemnation were piling up. Although the tablets helped slightly, because nothing around me changed (like my health and my emotional struggles), I was becoming more bound and entrenched in negative patterns of behaviour.

The local vicar and his wife had become friends with us. We spent many an evening chatting about doctrine over a curry. Eventually, I opened up to James, which was helpful to a point but we both felt, after a while, that we were just tickling the surface and not tackling the roots. So, James told me he wanted me to go and see another vicar he knew that was more experienced in trauma and abuse as he was a qualified counsellor. Initially, I felt disappointed and disillusioned as I'd dared to trust and bring the hurting me into the open... and, again, it wasn't working out. The thoughts of starting again with a stranger completely upskittled me but after talking to Geoff, I had a different perspective and, with his support, I went ahead and met Brett for counselling.

Brett was a gentle man and, although he made me feel as safe as possible, it took a long, long time to be able to fully open up and be honest. Brett didn't show any judgement and, on the contrary, he always concluded the sessions with how well I'd done and how amazed he was at how well I was doing on a day-to-day basis. His approval was something that deeply touched me and I was so grateful to God for bringing him across my path. Brett had a way of disarming a person and the hour's session flew by. It took many months to actually begin to get down to the real issues and they usually came out five minutes before the end of the session. I would beat about the bush as I hadn't got the bravery to be honest about what really hurt and how weak I really was.

After a year or, so Brett finally got out of me all that had happened and exactly how that was outworking itself in the present day. I went home so relieved and cried tears of joy that were so releasing. I'd finally got to the point where we could start to work through things bit-by-bit and see healing.

A couple of days later, the phone rang in the morning and, as usual, I didn't answer it as I had a thing about phones and hated talking on them, so Geoff answered it and I could tell I instantly that something was really wrong.

He slumped against the worktop in the kitchen and looked at me with an 'I'm so sorry, Pippa' look! What on earth had happened? I braced myself, and putting the phone down quietly, he burst into tears saying, "Pippa, Brett is dead!"

WHAT? NO! NOOO!

I had only seen him 36 hours ago. It was like someone had punched me in the stomach. I'd lost the man who had genuinely listened to me and actually helped me and I'd only just told him THE TRUTH! Now, he was gone! I was devastated. Life seemed so cruel!

After a couple of days of coming to terms with my loss, I took myself away and talked it all through with the Lord. I felt Him impress on my heart that although Brett was taken quickly and out of the blue, he'd not suffered and, in a moment, arrived in heaven to take his rest from all Earth's troubles! He had carried so many griefs and secrets that people had entrusted to him, and I remembered him once saying, "I will die taking so many secrets to the grave, so Pippa you can tell me anything!" He now had his peace, and it was his time to rest! I felt comforted.

The following Sunday came round quickly and the vicar's wife, Mel, came across to talk to me. Brett's passing was at the forefront of my mind, and I blurted out, "Oh Mel! Do you know that Brett has died?"

"I'd heard something," she replied. However, to my shock, she went on to say, "Well, Pippa. Maybe God removed him because you were becoming too dependent on him!" I had no words to respond. It felt like such a heartless thing to say. Didn't she know what I was dealing with? Obviously not!

Nevertheless, I chose to forgive her as I knew well that forgiveness is always the best option. I'd had to do it so many times, I was becoming rather an expert!

Chapter Thirteen
Runaway Train

Geoff and I had built a home that cultivated a heart to seek after God and I knew without a shadow of a doubt that the most important thing to me as a mother was that my children would love God from the depths of their being and find out what their purpose was for Him in this life. I was passionate in conveying this to them, but I found myself in a place where I felt lost and just tried to get through each day. The years of denial, trying to hide my feelings and trying to do what was right and please everyone while still trying to seek God left me exhausted and weak.

Who am I? How can I show others the truth yet be lost, myself? Inside, I was crying so much. "Please help me!" the little girl cried, inside.

It felt so good to deprive myself of food. It felt like a punishment! But who was I punishing and why? To be angry at myself felt good and yet it felt so wrong! I'd had so many years of other people telling me what I should and should not do, what I should and should not wear and how I should treat everyone around me. I had lost my identity and at times felt like a 'nobody'! The old feelings of being invisible haunted me again.

Auntie Glenda became more challenging than ever. She seemed to be paranoid and relentlessly complained about how often people were unkind to her. From my observations, she appeared to repel people through her desperation for acceptance and approval, causing those around her to withdraw as she required far more from a relationship than was necessary or healthy.

She was intense and 'in-your-face'. I loved Auntie Glenda, but I was increasingly realising that I needed to start to address MY needs and, although I needed to be gracious to her, she was starting to bring a heaviness and neediness that I could really do without.

I was drinking, starving myself then binging! Everything felt out of control. No one knew and I felt so alone. I had started to imagine what it would be like to hurt myself. The thought of hurting myself made something inside feel appeased and satisfied.

On the other hand, I felt ashamed and so guilty, too. The thoughts of having a physical wound was a recognition of the pain inside my heart. This seemed, at the time, like a good thing as other people might not see my pain but I could remind myself and it was an acknowledgment of it.

I was aware that deception was becoming part of my life as I covered up these issues and found myself 'acting' and leading people to believe I was somebody I wasn't. This wasn't me! This wasn't how God had made me and how I was brought up. It felt like I was on a runaway train that no one could stop.

In a way, I felt like I could totally empathise with the addict or the person who society rejected as I felt misunderstood and of no value. Addiction does not just affect the heroin addict or the alcoholic. It is a desperate need that anyone can have to satisfy something that hurts them, maybe even destroying them. It ravages your logic and your strength, takes everything from you and leaves you feeling like you owe it your life because you can't survive without it! Just as it warns against in the Bible, I did the things I shouldn't do and the things I should do, I avoided!

How did I end up in this place? Pushed, pulled and driven in so many directions; none of them what I wanted to choose but I didn't have the power to stop. On the one hand, I was such an open and transparent person, willingly sharing who I was and caring deeply for other people and seeing their value, but I had this other private side that felt damaged, hurt, hidden away and unable to make sense of things. I covered it all over with a big smile, distractions and lots of make-up.

I'd been blessed with a deeply forgiving heart which kept me free from some of the bondages that bitterness can bring and I wasn't one who held onto wounds by wanting the other person to suffer because of what they had done. But I had one belief system that I desperately needed God to break into and that was the belief that I was an unworthy failure and a deep disappointment to God.

It broke my heart to think that if my children knew, oh, how it would hurt them! And how confused would they feel? They would be disillusioned with me and everything I'd taught them. They would feel I'd been a hypocrite! Oh, how my heart hurt!

"Lord, You are my rock, and You are the Truth. Please help me to stand and live in your truth and freedom!" I ached and yearned for God to help me.

My battles were becoming more private and intense, with my mind a turbulent machine, creating wave-after-wave of self-hatred and disappointment. I still felt invisible, just as I had when I was a little girl. The perceptions of my past were becoming more and more distorted as I hadn't challenged my way of thinking and no one else had, either.

I yearned for attention and to be someone people liked and wanted to spend time with, thus had a poor lack of judgment at times and got myself into scrapes. My nature was bubbly and kind, and I would often put my trust in people too willingly, finding out too late that they had ulterior motives. I found myself being taken advantage of and was often unable to defend myself, struggling to stand up to people and say, "No!" being more upset about potentially upsetting them and offending them than I was about my own personal safety.

Fortunately, somehow, these incidents never did develop into anything serious.

I always wanted to please and would go to great lengths to help anyone with my time or money. Desperately, I tried to cover up the fact that I didn't feel well, and I found myself exhausted; stamina was never a strong point because of years of chronic illness. Never-ending cycles were rolling on. I always started off well because my heart so wanted to please God, then I burned myself out doing my absolute best as I'd not be able to sustain whatever I was trying to do; ultimately, I would feel I'd let *another* person down and, in doing so, let myself down, too! This just added to the self-hatred I already hauled around with me.

Mum was so funny, and her hilarious laughing was part of who I was but now I found myself in a place where things were no longer funny, and life seemed so serious and complicated. Mum said to me one day, "Pippa, I haven't heard you laugh for a long time!" It saddened me that Mum had noticed but I couldn't begin to explain why. I guess I couldn't articulate it as even I had forgotten the 'good old days'! Even during the abuse and illness all those years ago, I could still laugh... but now, I was weary.

If only I could connect with who I really was and if only I could connect with God! The next few years were what I'd describe as silent years as I closed myself off from God and my church friends, just focusing on getting through each day. The little girl inside was grieving. She'd lost so much. She'd lost her identity, she'd lost her ability to trust and she grieved to go back to 'before'! But 'before' was so long ago and how could this little girl ever regain what she had lost? It felt like my closest relative had died without saying goodbye!

....

The practice of going to see my doctor had become a drudgery and, although he wanted to see me regularly, I stayed away as much as possible. The endless hospital admissions had taken their toll on me, and I couldn't stand the thought of another arterial blood gas being taken and more time away from Geoff, the children and home.

What was the point in believing for healing from my breathing problems? I'd been let down and disappointed so many times! And I'd believed and even stopped all my medications! I'd run around the block to show I believed my lungs were healed... but all to no avail as I'd ended up back in hospital (my second home, as I called it).

Why should I trust God to mend my broken heart? So far, I'd offered Him all the pieces and I'd given Him permission to do whatever it took to mend me. But here I was: lonely, scared and in hiding. At least when you're hiding, no one expects anything from you, and you don't feel guilty because you're cut off from everyone.

Mondays were my favourite day but as each week wore on and the weekends approached, an anxiety started to build... and by Sunday mornings, I was desperately praying that I would be able to get through church without crying or making a fool of myself.

I began to resent the fact that people constantly remarked on what an amazing family we were and how they wished theirs was like ours. "They must be joking!" I said, silently to myself. My kids were amazing, and Geoff was doing his best under pressure, but I hated myself and resented the fact I was everything everyone else wanted me to be and now people were forming a judgement on how 'together' our family was, inferring that we were an example of a solid Christian family and that things looked easy! I did want people to believe the best, but how I ached to be respected while having someone acknowledge the pain and difficulties I was encountering.

To me, the whole meaning of being a Christian is to have a saviour who forgives our sins, setting us free from condemnation and a friend who sticks closer than a brother and a present help in time of any sort of need. All the years of mental toil, anguish and physical struggle had opened a doorway to so many bad things. I knew Jesus was the answer but accessing Him and being able to fully bring Him into this hurting area of my life was going to take time and a great deal of help and understanding.

Chapter Fourteen
Living in the Not Yet Rather than the Can't

Mum was approaching the end of her life, and this was going to be hard. She'd always been heavily involved in my life; she had looked after me so selflessly when I was a little girl, sitting up night in and night out trying to make me comfortable even though she wasn't. And now, although we didn't always see eye to eye, we spoke every day and she called every afternoon. We never had cross words because we knew how deeply we loved each other, and they weren't worth it. Without a doubt, her heart for me was that I would always love God and represent Him well, as she did in her own, simple way. She sincerely and conscientiously lived her life with a deeply thankful heart and a willingness to share the love of Jesus with whoever crossed her path! For that, I am so proud.

Mum had become quite reclusive, and she was struggling to look after herself, so it was the most natural thing to move her in to live with us. What didn't happen so easily was convincing her that her car license needed handing in. "Mum, you are eighty-eight and you've parked in the privet bush at the Methodist church, you've got stuck on an incline at major traffic lights with a row of thirty cars behind you, you have no paint on your wings and your car was the only one in Tesco that parked horizontally! Mother, its time!" She reluctantly agreed and we waved goodbye as Geoff drove the battered vehicle to the scrap yard.

She had cancer and I took great pride in making the end of her life as luxurious as possible, meeting her every need! Nothing was too much. In my mind, she was a piece of gold and

I looked after her with her knowing that. She described it as, "Living on the fat of the land," which gave me a beautiful sense of achievement and pride.

My precious mum passed away with me and Joey by her side. Every day, she had talked about wanting to be with Jesus and now she'd made it! I let out the deepest heartrending cry and felt like my insides had been ripped from me. I knew she had gone but she had been my security and I was now on my own, or so it felt. I kissed her so much and, overwhelmed with tears, I then chuckled as I wiped my furiously runny nose on her dressing gown that was wrapped so neatly round her. She was such a lady and that would have horrified her, but I guess the rebel in me found it a little funny!

The following few months were to be a relief as I didn't have to constantly consider my mum's needs, but I missed her terribly. I find myself adjusting to a life where I could be me without having to please Mum or look after her, but all the struggles of the years that had burdened me and had to be kept totally under wraps came tumbling out.

During the previous couple of years, I'd had occasional chats with my friend, Ann, about my struggles but we'd not fully discussed everything that was plaguing me. Somehow, it always felt too much to open up completely and tackle my pain as I felt I needed to be in control and hold it together. We had been to the same church, and both had a passion to know God and got excited talking about Him. I didn't want her to see the side of me that was weak, ungodly and a let-down, so the pain had deepened, and I'd taken on coping mechanisms that added more complexities which hindered me from reaching for healing. How on earth could I tell her the ungodly things I did to get through my dark times?

Mum was gone and all the pain came to the surface. All the need to protect Auntie Glenda in the past didn't seem a priority anymore. I couldn't hurt Mum with my pain now but I felt alone and trapped, not knowing how I could possibly make things right. I wanted to make sense of things and now seemed the right time to try. However, I felt let down by church leaders, my friends... and God!

Feelings of anger rumbled around me, and I occasionally imagined what it would be like to smash all the shop windows in the middle of town to get rid of my pent-up frustration but then I'd smile and acknowledge that I wasn't angry at local retailers, or a person or a group of people. It was just me with whom I was angry! Who on earth could I talk to? What Christian would be that understanding? This was my mess and only I could sort it!

We'd been part of a new church for a while now and everyone was so welcoming and wanted to involve me and Geoff in events in the church. There were lots of areas that needed pastoral care and lots of opportunities to get involved. The pressure inside me began to build as I couldn't hold together for much longer all the broken pieces inside. Monday mornings began to be a relief as church the day before was over and I could have a few days reprieve from trying to be something I felt I was not. The last thing I wanted was to show the pain inside to these lovely people. I didn't want to spoil what we appeared to have.

Every day, I cried for Mum. She'd left a hole in my life, and I felt like I needed a double cuddle! The little girl inside needed to be listened to and held and the adult me needed a connection that helped me feel safe and supported. "Jesus! Please help me! I cannot live like this any longer!" I desperately and earnestly cried out to God to give me strength to, one last time, dare to believe I could be healed fully and restored. "God, I need someone who will stick with me till I'm free and not give up on me or get sick of me before I reach the end!"

My friendship with Ann was deepening again and I often visited for a cuppa; she always produced a fresh cream cake, insisting that I had two! At that time, I was in a frame of mind that wanted to starve myself and eating her two cream cakes was a real challenge!

On this particular Tuesday night, we sat with a cuppa, a cream cake and our feet on Ann's leather chairs that ejected an elevated footrest as you pulled a lever. It was lethal if you didn't get it right as it shot out and whipped you backwards, without warning! This night, I pulled the lever and, in a flash, I shot backwards, legs in the air and my cup of tea splattered all over the floor!

After the mop-up, we launched once again into the subject of Uncle Ivan. As we talked about it, Rob (her husband) walked into the lounge. We both clammed up and looked at each other. Rob said, "Oh, I'm sorry. I obviously walked in at the wrong moment!"

"No, no. It's ok," I said. For some reason, I wanted Rob to know. I'd battled for so long to keep this thing under wraps and now I'd found two friends who I trusted and needed.

I looked to Ann who said, "Shall I tell him?" I responded with a yes and quickly put my head down as I felt ashamed and embarrassed as to what was about to come out of Ann's mouth. She said, "Pippa's uncle did unmentionable things to her and she's struggling to deal with it!"

Rob sat down. He was silent yet looked believing and he had a sad look in his eye. He didn't seem to want to get out of the room quickly or change the subject, which surprised me. Maybe he actually cared and wanted to help! We spent the next hour talking about the past and how Uncle Ivan had had a damaging impact on my life. This was significant in the unpicking of the sequence of events and the trauma that was attached to them.

Could this be possible? Could God have actually given me some people who would help me and stick with me? I held this thought at arms-length as it would only be the test of time that would determine the outcome.

In a strange way, Rob was a presence in the room that helped me! I didn't trust men's motives and to talk to them, especially about *the subject*, would normally have been one I'd have to weigh up and build myself up for over a long time. I deeply trusted Ann and, somehow, it helped me to trust Rob. In my opinion, just because a couple *seemed* ok, it certainly didn't mean that it was the case behind the scenes. Several of the people that hurt me were 'respected' people and appeared to have good marriages. However, Rob had always been incredibly respectful towards me, and, because of his quiet way, it somehow helped me to relax around him. It wasn't until much later in our friendship that I realised that Rob was very much like my precious Dad. Rob, like my Dad, was perfectly happy to sit for long enough and not speak. He was content and didn't waste his words but when he did speak, it was worth a listen... and if he was talking about God, he was on point.

Even though I'd quickly reached a point where I could talk to Rob about the past, it was still going to take some time to fully trust him. But he definitely had a head start and that was due to God.

Without realising it at the time, I desperately missed my dad and now my mum had gone, the little girl inside me was lost and felt so alone. In a way, it was like I'd been given a foster mum and dad. We joked about it and when I went to visit, Geoff would say, "Off to see your mum and dad again?" It was so funny as I was the oldest and they certainly didn't look like my mum and dad! Even though I was in my forties, God had seen the need to give me two people who were safe, honest, understanding and knew what unconditional love was. Two people who could walk, talk and carry me through as I faced the traumas of my past.

The biggest challenge, at that point, was the need to feel safe! But deep inside, no matter how Geoff protected me and how safe things were around me, I always felt on high alert. Going away from home was terrifying. Everyone has holidays and days away but for me, it stirred something inside that felt sick and fearful. New settings with new people were a challenge, too, as I couldn't relax and was never sure what would happen or if I was safe. I knew that I needed to open up and be honest, in fact, I knew I needed to tell everything. Over the years, I'd try to talk about what had happened, but it was like a huge blanket was thrown over my thoughts and I felt like I was choking. The trauma prevented me from talking. This time, I decided that, regardless of how I felt or how I physically reacted, I was going to attempt to open up and be honest.

It was a strange thing but, as we sat talking, I felt I couldn't proceed without saying to Rob, "Rob whilst I'm talking to you, you're not a man...just a friend." Rather bizarrely, for me to be able to talk through what Uncle Ivan had done, I couldn't bear the thought of Rob being a man, so by denying myself those thoughts, I was able to talk to them both.

No one around me knew what I was going through, but I certainly knew! I couldn't eat properly, and I was stressed when I had to eat in front of people. Everyone thought I was succeeding on my new-found diet as weight was dropping off me. When anyone challenged it, I felt angry and confused! Angry, because I didn't want anyone telling me anymore what to do. I wanted to be in control. Confused, as I felt deeply sad as I just felt disdain towards myself.

Rob and Ann set up a group chat on WhatsApp which meant that at any time I could text if I needed help or just a friendly voice. They would be there! This was a life saver and if Ann wasn't available, Rob was. They were there to reinforce what we'd talked about, and they both constantly reminded me that I was safe and valued. They must have said it a hundred times and each time as if it was the first time!

The first thing I noticed that impacted me was that Rob and Ann believed me! They not only believed me, but they were insistent that I wasn't guilty and Ann, in particular, was mad at Uncle Ivan! Somehow, it felt good that someone was angry and not initially forgiving. Although my mum and dad had forgiving hearts, it would have been healing for me, in the long term, if they'd prosecuted and acknowledged that what had happened was a crime! Geoff would have been mad in the past if I'd have let him, but I couldn't cope with how that would have outworked itself. Geoff is no small man, and one punch would have given him his own prison sentence.

The more I said to Ann, the more she wanted to get in the car and go and challenge him. Probably thump him, too, if it was allowed! Rob was the voice of reason, and he didn't say a lot but that was ok. In a fresh light, they helped me see that what had happened was a criminal act and I shouldn't disregard that. "That's something we can face if we need to," said Ann.

I CAN'T DO THIS! I'd opened up this can of worms, and I desperately want to shove them all back in the can but I couldn't!

I'd just had a hospital appointment and that was the last thing on my mind. I felt scared and couldn't stop the flashbacks and the video tape kept rolling.

Group chat: *Is anyone in? Please can I call for coffee? Feeling rubbish!*

Reply: *Kettle on! See you soon!*

Rob opened the door, and I couldn't look in his face. I felt ashamed and nervous. We sat in the lounge in my designated chair. It was the same one each time. I had chosen it. It needed to be in full view of the door so, if I needed it, I could have a quick getaway! I had my cushion, too! This protected me and I held it like my life depended on it!

"I can't go on! I can't do this!"

"Yes, you can!" said Rob. "Right now, you're living in the 'not yet' rather than the 'can't'" He always believed in me; they both did. I certainly didn't. I'm not sure what they saw but it certainly wasn't who I could see.

Chapter Fifteen
Power to Reframe Your Story

"Please can I tell you more?" I cried over the phone to Ann. It was like an explosion had gone off and I desperately needed to clean it up! A barrage of memories. A video playing. Vivid flashbacks and endless reminders of events. Before I could sort out the mess, I had to identify and fix the source. Years of ignoring it had only caused the crying that went on inside me to deepen and continue.

"Yes, of course; come round!" said Ann, without hesitation.

"But I need to tell you about the actual events!" My voice trembled and I felt sick in my stomach.

"Pippa, there is nothing you can tell us that will change our opinion of you, and you have the freedom to say anything and everything. You are safe and you are valued."

A wave of relief washed over me along with a foreboding and dread. What if my choking thing happens? What if I can't speak and I humiliate myself?

"Just come round and let's just take things steady and see what happens."

I arrived, got in the 'hot seat', pulled the lever and out shot the footrest. Cushion firmly hugged to my chest, cuppa in hand and... I couldn't speak! After a good few minutes, Ann said, "It's ok. Take your time."

I proceeded with immense caution. In an agitated tone, I said, "Please can I tell you exactly what happened?" I completely understood that no one likes to talk about the 'nitty gritty' of sexual abuse, but I knew that by refusing to talk, it just kept the secret going which made me feel even more dirty, as if my speaking about it should make me be more ashamed. Rob and Ann understood that I needed to tell someone and, in talking through it, it would off-load a very heavy burden. They could also give me a healthy perspective and challenge damaging ideas that I had about myself and people around me and my wrong perceptions of the people who had hurt me.

So, I launched into it, stuttering and stammering all the way! I looked intently at Rob as I felt on very high alert! He didn't seem to blink or move a muscle. That helped me as the horrid stuff I was saying didn't seem to cause him to react with disdain or repulsion. I had his full attention without judgement. Ann looked deeply concerned and was very defensive of me in her demeanour; her reactions, too, were exactly what I needed. For once, I felt defended. They listened intently and gave me a platform where I knew I could be raw in my honesty, and it felt good to have people who obviously thought a detestable injustice and crime had been committed against me. My own mum and dad's reaction and other people's had never given me that impression. It wasn't Mum or Dad's fault entirely, though, as I never gave them the full picture of what really happened.

As I relayed the full details of what Uncle Ivan had done, the anguish and fear welled up like a volcano. I sobbed incessantly and then, in a flash, jumped to my feet, causing Rob and Ann to jump too! This was to become a recurring reaction as I could only survive saying small chunks of information before having a physical reaction and having to get out of the room quickly. Each time, I ran to the bathroom and locked the door where I could throw up and give the anxiety level a chance to even out. Walking back into the room wasn't easy as part of me felt horrified at what I'd just shared with my friends. During the next couple of hours, the stubborn part of me reared its head. I always felt angry and disagreeable even if they didn't notice, but it was always directed towards myself.

"Pippa, none of what Uncle Ivan did was your fault and you weren't responsible for the other men that hurt you, either!"

I tried to explain why I hadn't been able to defend myself or get away as a child. "But I couldn't speak! I tried! I tried so hard to, but only a tiny squeak came out! I couldn't move; my legs were like lead and I couldn't do what I wanted or needed to do! I'm so stupid! I'm a piece of rubbish!"

I was in my own world at this point, barely able to take on board what was being said. This type of conversation was repeated over and over until, eventually, the truth began to sink in. Slowly but surely, the penny dropped. None of it was my choice! I had never given consent and the events were so upsetting that the only way my mind could preserve itself was to close down, as fear had caused me to be unable to speak or move. This was not a proof of guilt in any way!

Ann constantly reminded me that I was a very young child, and he was a man in his forties and that the full weight of guilt was on his shoulders. As for the other men, they were adults and in no way was I responsible! I was vulnerable and no one had any right to take advantage of that!

Throughout all this unpicking of wool (that's just how it felt: a mass of wool, completely tangled and knotted), the crying inside was unbearable. A silent little girl was screaming and crying. Deep inside, the tears were flowing... but not on the outside.

I cried out to Jesus, "Lord, what is happening inside?"

The next day, as I was sitting on my bedroom floor with my back against the wall, I suddenly heard the Lord say, "Your tears are 'soul tears'!"

"What are they, Lord?" I'd never heard of such a thing.

"These are the ones that are cried in deep distress, without recognition and they are cried inside the soul, unable to be let out."

It made complete sense to me, immediately. "Yes, Lord. That's right! They go on day and night with no outlet! Please can you release them?"

I knew, from that point onwards, that my tears would be seen and would be caught, and God certainly had given me the right people to lead me into that. It became very clear that over the next few months, God had given me Rob and Ann; in essence, Him saying, "I see you, I hear you, I believe you and I will comfort you." That was life changing because it wasn't just them acknowledging it, it was God saying it to me, too.

There were the most wonderful pockets of revelation that popped up here and there and Rob and Ann were doing a superb job of giving me time and listening ears. But the majority of the time I felt confused, and my emotions were battered from pillar to post.

The evenings were the worst and, as they approached, I couldn't hold inside all the grief and anguish. I couldn't sleep but it was all I wanted to do. I tried desperately to bring peace into my mind but I couldn't seem to access it so I threw myself into drawing portraits. Earphones on. Volume high! I listened to hours of worship music: songs that spoke of God's immense grace and love. The tears flowed and flowed. I could feel God's love but it didn't seem to be able to penetrate my heart. There was a vicious conflict between truth and lies. At this point, I was believing more lies than truth and I was trying desperately to get away from myself. Wine was my friend: we liked each other, it was always available, it helped me let go, it encouraged me to hate myself and it said, "Yes, go on... if you want a late-night walk, why not?" It wasn't a friend of reason any more than I was, so we got on... or so I thought!

When everyone was tucked up in bed, out I would go, walking in the fields and lonely places. I didn't care if it was unsafe. I wasn't safe anyway and I felt of no value! Desperately trying not to ring Rob or Ann for help, I walked and walked. Finally, slumping down on the ground, I grabbed my phone many times and texted my new 'mum and dad'. They navigated me through some of my toughest times very late at night whilst everyone else was in bed and I was out down a dark lane. "I can't go on! I'm scared and confused, and I hate who I am!"

"Pippa, no matter how you feel, you are LOVED, and you are SAFE now." We had arguments over going back home but Ann always won by saying, "Right, I'm coming over!"

"NO WAY!" I'd quickly retort. I couldn't let her see me like that.

She'd stay on the phone with me until I was safely home. Flopping into bed, exhausted, my sleep was troubled as my fears and anxieties washed over me. But at least another day was over.

My story had remained the same for many years but now it was being unpicked, challenged and redefined. It felt like it had taken on a life of its own. No longer could I contain it neatly or speak about it like it was happening to someone else. My story was now a book I wanted to get rid of but because of a loving husband, true friends and a wonderful Saviour who heals, I was beginning to reframe my story.

As a little girl, I used to lie on my bed and fantasise what it would be like if I could speak, if someone would listen. I had decided that one day I would write a book and, because no one saw my pain, I would give it the title, "I'M ALRIGHT. I'M ONLY HURTING". I had felt that hurting meant nothing, didn't count and wasn't important. So, I would always say I was alright even when I was hurting. Tears had rolled down my cheeks as I had sat cross-legged on my bed, crying deeply without making a single sound - I had learnt that trick a long time ago!

I had loved writing the things Jesus said to me. I had written lots of little poems about Him and, that day, I wrote a letter to Him.

It was MY story... and now, I had the title! I told Jesus all about my pain and explained how confused and scared and lonely I was. In my childlike way, I unfolded my thoughts and, in total sincerity, brought my letter before Him.

Little did I know that years later, as an adult, I would find myself writing a letter back to that broken little girl, speaking words of love, truth and healing.

As the weeks rolled into months, I found myself questioning if I'd ever be free from torment. The weekly sessions of talking to 'Mum and Dad', the texts, the late-night conversations, the dropping by for strong coffee and a chat all made me think that if there was no good reason for this, and if nothing good can be brought out of it, what was the point in living? I needed another revelation from God!

"Lord I need to see above all this filth and all this damage. I want You to show me what was happening in the spiritual realm whilst this natural thing was happening. I want You to show me if there was any purpose that You intended to come out of this thing!"

Immediately, I saw myself as a really small child. I could see what Uncle Ivan was doing but that wasn't where my gaze went! Oh my goodness! Behind the little girl, I saw a HUGE angel kneeling and his HUGE wings were beginning to open. He was poised, ready to fly and jump into action to rescue me. As this picture was before me, I physically felt a breeze as I spiritually watched his wings moving.

As I continued to look, I spotted squares: gold squares. In fact, they were everywhere! They covered the floor, the walls and the whole room where Uncle Ivan was hurting me. In each square was a face: someone who was broken and abused and abandoned. God spoke to me and said, "My heart broke as I saw you! But because of what you have endured, I am giving you people like squares of gold. You will gather them and restore them and heal them. You are going to go into the darkest places to look for people who have been given up on by others."

I continued to observe that Jesus was right by my side; He wasn't turning away - He was praying for me and talking to His Father in heaven. I certainly wasn't alone, and He clearly spoke again: "You were damaged and broken but you weren't destroyed. He took your body and damaged your soul, but your spirit belonged to Me, and I never allowed our love to be separated."

With great joy, I shared this with Rob and Ann, they were so pleased, and Rob had one of his brain waves: "I know, let's call our group chat, 'Golden Squares'!" To this day, that's what it remains.

New challenges were emerging with the need to change my approaches, reactions and responses. This was no easy task as I had no idea that some things *needed* to change! I was beginning to feel a distance growing between myself and Auntie Glenda and I was growing anxious about her visiting. What if Uncle Ivan dropped her off?

I felt a fear of him and a repulsion that I'd not felt before. If he came, he would kiss me and hug me! "Well, that's ok, it's got to be," I said to Ann. I needed them to know it was all ok and I would just handle it to keep the peace.

"No, you don't have to kiss and hug him! It's not ok!" said Ann. "They need to know things have changed! You have changed and you now recognise what is not good or healthy for you!"

I decided I needed to confront Uncle Ivan in some way so, with a deep breath and my heart thumping out of my chest, I rang him. "Hello. Is that Uncle Ivan? It's Pippa."

He replied in a surprised voice and immediately asked, "Are you ok? Is something wrong?"

I spluttered and replied, "Well to be honest, I'm not too good as I'm trying to piece together what you did to me, and I need you to know that it's knocked my confidence and given me anxieties and fears that I'm struggling to come to terms with."

He appeared to respond very kindly and out of concern. But it wasn't long before he started to justify his acts by explaining how I had triggered in him memories of *his* abuse because, according to him, I looked like his abuser. Because he thought I looked like his abuser, he, in a warped way, excused himself by saying that I had caused his sexual feelings. He continued to describe what his babysitter had done to him when he was a child, quickly being absorbed in his own story rather than acknowledging what I was trying to say. He was trying to deflect the issue by focusing on the fact that we both had a story to tell and had something in common without giving any credence to the fact that he was the guilty party in mine.

All I had done was act like any normal child, yet he took the opportunity to act on his unrestrained feelings and excuse himself by putting the blame onto me. In his manipulative manner, he said I shouldn't blame myself... but he certainly didn't blame himself either! He truly believed that all his actions were the fault of HIS abuser! At least I knew where he stood and I ended the call graciously but knowing that he wasn't to be trusted and, as ever, he had failed to take any responsibility. He made absolutely sure I understood that this conversation was just to be between us and that Auntie Glenda must never know.

It was only now that I could really start to see the manipulation, coercion and lying that was part of his life and that I had been drawn into it by birth and his wrong choices.

Chapter Sixteen
Truth Over Feelings

Golden squares chat: *Ann! Are you there?*

She must be at work, I thought, but it wasn't long before Rob answered: *Are you ok, Pippa?*

I can't sort my mind out. It's all jumbled up!

Rob did his usual *'Kettle's on!'* comment and that was my invitation to go round.

I had started to notice that I was increasingly feeling confused and under a lot of pressure. This made me feel isolated from everyone. To most people, the number of times they repeated the same old things that I needed to hear would have seemed a waste of time but to me, it was a life saver and, even if Ann and Rob were frustrated or tired of the repetition, they certainly never showed it. I guess it was like where you repeatedly tell a child something until, eventually, it lodges, and they remember and act on what they have been taught.

I'd got into my head that, underneath it all, I was just an object. How could anyone argue that point? "My feelings didn't count, and I meant nothing when Uncle Ivan acted towards me the way he did," I insisted.

"Pippa, how can his actions determine your value?" Rob was firm and couldn't be convinced otherwise. I had battled through childhood with the loneliness of illness and feelings of objectification from hospitalisation and not only Uncle but other men thinking I was someone they could use for their pleasure! So, regardless of what my friends said, my conclusion was that I was nothing more than an object!

I couldn't break through! I couldn't accept that the worthlessness I felt wasn't justified! Rob acknowledged that

Uncle Ivan and others were only thinking about themselves, but their issues were not mine to own. "What about who Jesus says you are? Are you going to listen to Jesus or the lies?"

I felt annoyed and irritated by his black-and-white stance! "But it's not that simple!" I argued.

"Yes, it is!" he argued back. I held my cushion to my chest like my life depended on it. I wanted to run out of that room and run and run and never come back. Rob had challenged the very core of me! He refused to see it the way I saw it.

"But so much was taken from me: all the good, all purity and the nice me!" I looked at my arms and hands, they looked dirty to me, in fact, all of me did! "Can't you see that?" I said, with desperation.

"I understand your feelings but, Pippa, the Truth is what will set you free! Why did Jesus die? Is His blood not enough to wash you?"

I couldn't look in his eyes. I didn't want to agree! I felt ashamed and belittled. I wanted him to agree that I was an object. I felt so rubbish at that moment that I even wanted my friend to accept that I had been wrong and that I was no good. The thoughts of someone hurting me and punishing me felt normal and that was where I often went to in my mind when I couldn't get peace.

We both agreed that this was a good time for a coffee break! Normally, I was a white-and-no-sugar-in-my-tea type of person but this time, I needed something stronger! "Rob, can I have a strong coffee with a sugar?" He drank coffee like treacle, which looked horrid, but during these sessions, it became highly appealing to me, too.

Rob was resolute in his belief that things were going well, and we were making progress. I wasn't so convinced. I wanted to be 'oven-ready' like a chicken and not one that needed all the preparation. I was realising that growth and comfort together didn't exist and that it takes courage to grow through what you go through. To move forward and learn as you go is hard, challenging and uncomfortable. I kept making the same mistakes as I seemed as weak as a kitten. In the past, I'd always prided myself on being strong in so many ways yet how did I stop my mind from replaying, over and over again, the things that happened so long ago? It was like I was frozen, emotionally, in that time. It didn't seem fair that the problem didn't originate from me, yet I was the only one who could change it.

"What if I'm running out of time? What if, suddenly, they've all had enough and aren't willing to help me anymore?" These thoughts often came after a traumatic session or when I thought I'd overstepped a mark with something I'd said. It felt like a race against the clock. Just as Jesus was right at the centre, helping me to come to terms with everything and helping me navigate through it all, so the enemy of my soul was there too, doing the exact opposite! After all, even though people had hurt me by their terrible choices, it was the sin and destruction that Satan had planned all along. He knew I belonged to Jesus and that my heart was His, so the battle was fierce over who I was going to believe and how willing I was going to be to choose the life and freedom that Jesus was offering me. Satan was not letting go without a battle and I was in the middle, afflicted by my experiences but knowing there was a higher calling. If I could truly take hold of it, all these shackles would break off and fall to the ground. Even something bad and ugly can be something you carry around as a friend because you've never known time without it and it appears to be part of you. "Please give me more time!" I pleaded as if my life depended on it, but my friends always calmly said that I could have as much time as I needed and that they would not leave me

I needed a miracle! But I was very aware that to get a miracle, there were often difficulties leading up to it. I was sick of the difficulty and the struggle. In my determination to show no signs of struggle to the outside world, my stubbornness and unyielding unwillingness to let go was thriving. As this was growing, I could see it but felt scared to acknowledge it as I knew a point would come when I had to lay everything down. I knew that submitting to God was the most important way to live but I felt unworthy and too far gone to believe that there was a way back to salvation.

In a strange way, I felt responsible for all the bad things that had happened to me and yet couldn't see that I was responsible for my reactions to all those things. My reactions and lifestyle were a form of self-punishment, and it was only me, Ann and Rob that were aware of it. What harm was there in that?

Church wasn't just a building that I went to out of religious duty. I knew that I was part of the church and the whole group of believers together made it complete. The church building only facilitates the meeting together of the true church and it needs all of us together. Someone is the eye and someone else the arm, figuratively speaking! Whatever I was, I knew I was letting my part of it down.

I thought about all the people I could help and encourage but whilst I was in that state, I felt of no use to anyone. I was like a disabled body part. How could it be, then, that God chose to be so relentlessly kind, gracious and forgiving towards me? Without fail, God would - in so many varying ways - try to speak to me whilst I attended church most weeks. Whether or not I was listening was another matter!

"Oh, no!" I uttered under my breath as a family member invited me to a ladies' conference at her church. How could I say no? She really wanted me there with her! Overcoming an aggravated inward battle, I accepted. As I drove there the following weekend, I felt annoyed with myself; I'd put a lot of effort into putting on my make-up, but it was vanishing quickly. Tears engulfed me and I sobbed, crying out to God to help me and set me free.

The tissue I'd been using had disintegrated into a billion fibres, was saturated and shredded and sticking to my jumper.

The idea of arriving looking nice, in control and 'together' was rapidly disappearing!

As the day began, all the ladies sang with gusto and obvious excitement. However, I felt uncomfortable and all I wanted to do was go home, be on my own and drink copious amounts of tea. Each chair had a little goody-bag on it containing a chocolate, a candle and a tiny notebook and pen to jot down what God was saying during the day. I was surprised and, again, softened by the love of God who had evidently seen my heart, identifying some of my areas of pain. The notebook came in very handy!

The following words are exactly what I wrote in the notebook as said by different people who were sharing what they thought God wanted to say:

Does fear rule you? God has provided a way out. Confess your sins or the things that eat away at you. How do you get rid of your pain: bury it or withdraw or run? It can only be healed through obedience. Jesus is the advocate, and we need to be honest. Does hiding satisfy? Are you trying to stay safe? Do you feel safe? To fear is not of God but to fear God is wisdom. There's no condemnation for those in Christ. I see this in your life; it's too much of a load to bear! Use your voice and confess the load; the light is coming!

The journey home was similar to the journey going - lots of tears and shredded tissues - but minus the anguish. God had spoken and I had listened. God had clearly told me that it was ok to talk... in fact, it was what He wanted me to do! Rob and Ann were delighted that I'd been given confirmation to continue sharing my pain but also been given confirmation that there would be a light at the end of the tunnel and that healing was on its way.

The first part of the ladies' day had been about feeling safe and secure. This was certainly the phase I was about to embark on with Rob and Ann as no matter what happened, I always had an underlying feeling of being unsafe and struggled to know who I could trust.

"You are safe and valued!" There it was again! Every time I wobbled, those two truths were repeated.

"But how can you say that? You don't know that!"

Somehow, I'd adopted the view that 'value' wasn't really worth anything. They were saying that I was valued but what difference did it make? It didn't alter the past or make me safe, so value accounted for nothing. Object versus value seemed to have the same outcome! If a bad person wants to hurt someone for their own pleasure or need, the person's value has absolutely no power to stop it. Therefore, the object is never safe, regardless of their value!

The longer this mental argument prevailed, the darker things felt. I just couldn't hear what God was trying to say. He spoke clearly but my hearing was dim. I was like the dear old lady who was as deaf as a door post and owned her own hearing aids but refused to wear them as she was adamant that they didn't help. The brain takes many weeks of constant bombardment to hear and connect with new signals but, just like some old ladies, I wasn't consistent in listening to the truth so even though it was spoken regularly and clearly, I didn't give it chance to resonate and build new patterns of thinking. I was terrified to trust and change my ways of thinking. I believed that it made me more vulnerable, contrary to Rob and Ann's beliefs. When trust has been broken on so many levels, how could the best thing be to TRUST again? It made no sense at all!

"I'm not going to church today," I said to Ann. In her usual tone, she very kindly but firmly said, "Oh, but just think what you might miss? God usually talks to you so I wouldn't miss it if I were you!"

Of course, she was right; she usually was! I could feel a lump in my throat as the assistant pastor (my good friend, Dex) must have written his sermon just for me: *There will never be a time or season when He forgets about you! Someone here is going through some distressing and challenging stuff! There is nothing He won't tear down for you. He will pursue you and not let you go and He will fight for you because the depth of His love for you is deeper than you can see at the moment."*

Again! He sees me! And in that moment, yet again, I heard the truth: if my value, my identity and the God of all creation were fighting for me then maybe, just maybe, I should fight harder and listen! My spirit was being challenged and was starting to grow... and so was my desire for God. I'd always deeply loved Him but, at times, the walls of my heart were so high, I didn't let Him in.

The tears that I was crying were starting to change and I realised that they were no longer 'soul tears' trapped with no outlet. These tears felt different, like they were washing me. I looked at my hands and body and thought, "Could it be possible that He's cleansing me? Could it be real that I'm beginning to feel clean? Dare I believe it?" And the more I questioned it, the greater the feeling grew. All the talks with Rob and Ann had laid a foundation deep in my mind that, at the time, I couldn't accept but now the Spirit of God had taken hold of this part of me, and a miracle was happening. The change no one else, nor I, could do; only God. Again, I remembered the great sacrifice that Jesus made when He died on the cross. He was humiliated and broken, had borne my shame all those years ago and He had been waiting, all along, to lift it off me!

I was realising the truth that we get more of whatever we magnify. It was an obvious analogy but to switch from magnifying what I thought I'd become to who and what God had made me was not that easy. Even if I wasn't dirty or guilty anymore, how on earth could I live in this new way of thinking with a confidence and self-esteem that felt shattered? I knew exactly what I wanted to say and had my own opinions but when it came to expressing them or myself, I crumbled inside, big-style! I'd had a life of illness, abuse and too many demands from people with opposite opinions.

Although truth was starting to take root, it didn't take much to appear to shake it. I didn't seem to have the strength or will to reject all the lies when they came along in their different forms. Auntie Glenda seemed to be more regular in her contact and, out of sheer coincidence, she FaceTimed at all the wrong moments. This made me feel angry at myself because, again, I would be chatting as if everything was fine whilst inside, I was battling, feeling silenced and unable to defend myself.

Boundaries were something that I needed to acknowledge and set but I didn't seem to be able to put my needs above everybody else's, minimising them. In the case of Auntie Glenda, I particularly struggled as I felt that I owed her so much. Because I was talking to Rob and Ann about her, I felt that I was betraying her... although, I couldn't deny the fact that I WAS beginning to notice that despite the fact that I was always sensitive to her feelings, she never reciprocated. She never picked up on my cues and always pressurised me into doing things her way. She loved me and wanted to spend time with me, but it had to be on her terms. If I happened to say that I could only see her on the Monday, she would ask to come on the Saturday. I would go on to try and explain that I had other plans but, for Auntie Glenda, that was a rejection and there was an unwritten rule that I should make her my priority.

Geoff was sick of it and the kids were disgruntled by her behaviour. Why couldn't I stand up for myself? I was scared of things getting out of control and upsetting the apple cart. After all, it was my duty to keep the peace... or so I thought, until Rob and Ann began to uncover the truth of how unacceptable this situation was.

It wasn't long before Auntie caused a reaction, once again! This time, I managed to not only stick up for myself, but told her what I expected from her in the future. We had been chatting on FaceTime and she started to talk about her and

Uncle Ivan's previous evening's television viewing. She proceeded to talk about the documentary they had watched, on Joseph Fritzl. He was a man who imprisoned his daughter and, over many years, physically and sexually abused her.

Auntie Glenda was incensed by his actions, and, in an abhorrent tone, she went on to say how unbelievable it was that Joseph's wife didn't know anything about it and that she couldn't understand how he could have done such a terrible thing! Something began to rise up in me and she went on to talk about their discussions over it. How could she not see what she was doing? How on earth did it not enter her head that Uncle Ivan had done to me some of the things that she was so upset about? How could she be so insensitive? My face had dropped and anyone else would have noticed. In a moment, I cancelled the call while Auntie was in mid-flow. This was something that I would normally find the height of rudeness and would never do! I immediately texted her, explaining, "*I did end the call as I couldn't listen any longer to what you were saying. Because of what Uncle Ivan had done to me, how could you talk about Joseph Fritzl's crimes as if they were different? From now on, please don't talk about anything on this subject and from this point, I don't want any references to Uncle in any way. However you do it is fine but make sure I never have to see him again!*"

It was almost a whole day before she replied: "*Pippa, I could do without what you said. I'm an innocent in all this. I knew nothing. It was a long time ago and it's not fair bringing all this up as things have been hard for me. I wished I'd have never mentioned Joseph Fritzl!*" I was upset and felt betrayed by her reply. After all, hadn't I always considered her feelings? Couldn't she have considered mine? For once, couldn't it have been about ME? But no, it couldn't, as Auntie Glenda could only see her own needs.

Regardless of that, I had achieved something: I had set a boundary and expressed myself honestly. My self-confidence muscles were beginning to flex, and it felt good!

Chapter Seventeen
Blackpool Donkey

Oh boy, was I missing my mum! Every time I passed the toiletries section in Tesco, the strong, perfumed aroma got me as it reminded me of her last few weeks when we used those products on her. "One day, it will be a happy reminder - not one that causes a need to take a deep breath," I thought to myself. I was still feeling lost as she'd gone and was never coming back. It seemed like the rest of the family had moved on and expected me to have done so by now... but they didn't know everything that I was dealing with. This seemed to be the story of my life: I never told people everything as I was worried that I was in the wrong, that I wouldn't be believed or was concerned that I wouldn't be able to handle other people's reactions.

It was time to open up to my family and I felt that the chronic shame that had held me for so long was no longer there. If I didn't make a choice to tell them then, it almost certainly would come out of my mouth at some point anyway, as this seemed to be the way things were moving forward. Whatever the inhibitor was in the past, it had gone. Rob and Ann had certainly drilled into me the fact that my story was up to me to tell, that I should never be ashamed and that if I needed to talk about it, I should. After all, I was realising that none of it had been my choice, that I had actually been brave and that everything I'd done was to protect myself and those around me.

While I was deciding how and when to tell my family, the topic of 'consent' was something that took up some time in the 'sessions' with strong coffee and my trusted cushion! Although I had thought I'd understood it, as we started to unpick the topic, I started to realise that in an abusive relationship with a child, the adult holds so much power, manipulation and coercion that the small mind of the child in some way feels to blame, feels responsible and confused over where their loyalties lie. I had truly believed that Uncle Ivan had loved me and hadn't wanted to hurt me so in that case, my pleas of, "NO, I don't like it!" and my, "NO! Please don't!" didn't count. I had justified it as me just me saying how I felt but because it seemed like he knew better, I had thought that I was misguided because he cared about me. So, it had felt like my NO shouldn't be my choice. What did I know?

To anyone else, consent sounds like a clear 'YES' or 'NO' but to me, it seemed different. I didn't understand consent because as a child as I had said, "No!" but it wasn't what I got. Every time I heard the word 'consent' as I grew up, I felt angry and agitated.

Ann got the brunt of it as I argued with her logic and, in an unusual setting, we eventually did iron it out. We were on a trip to Northern Ireland for a few days and sat in the back of a car. Someone in the car was writing a dissertation on consent and brought up the subject in general conversation. A horrid feeling started to rise in my throat! How could I give my opinion? My take on it felt different and, oh, I wished I could have shared it. I couldn't hold back anymore and had to tell Ann, who was sitting next to me, that I couldn't cope with this conversation. We couldn't speak as we were in close proximity to the other passengers, so we just started texting back and forth, back and forth, and eventually everything was said. Without frills and too many words, somehow the penny dropped.

No is no whether it be shouted or whispered. No one has the right to overpower someone else physically or emotionally in order to perform any sexual act with them that they don't want to do. And there is NEVER an occasion when an adult has any right to touch a child sexually even if the child is coerced into agreeing verbally. It is the sole responsibility of any adult having the care of any child to keep them safe and it's their job to overcome any weaknesses they might have to avoid them bringing harm to that child. I got it and it empowered me to be me and not what other people wanted me to be... of course, with one exception: Jesus! I wanted to please Him above everyone, and I knew He certainly wouldn't control or manipulate me into anything.

Shortly after this, a preacher from Toronto came to visit England and I decided to go along to one of his meetings. What an exciting and challenging message! The free, happy side of me rejoiced and hung off every word he was saying but the sad, troubled side of me felt downcast because even though I agreed with everything he was saying, something inside halted me, saying, "How can you fully receive this? You're too damaged!"

The opportunity arose for prayer, and I threw caution to the wind and went forward. What did I have to lose? Will, the preacher, bent down and whispered in my ear, "One day, I see you standing on the street corners with the abused and traumatised. You will be there to pull them out!"

I crumbled to the floor and wept. God, yet again, had seen me and He knew I couldn't see beyond the place I was in. So, in His kindness, He showed me a glimpse of the future. My heart received the insight that Will had been given. It reminded me of the 'golden squares'. All those people who were lost and had been trapped in abuse, yet God saw them and their value, and I would be someone who would help to lift them out. God had reconfirmed that, despite of all this pain, true freedom would come and not just for myself but many others.

Despite God giving me these repeated reminders of what my future held, the following months were a hard slog, as if I was trudging through treacle with stuff sticking to me as I walked along. They weren't new things, but they were new to *my* consciousness. As each part of my past was being worked through, another one seemed to take my attention. To me, this seemed like a backward step each time, but Rob and Ann constantly reiterated that it was a process and that we were definitely making progress. I was tired, I felt different from everyone around me and as the evenings approached, I dreaded them. I knew this was partly because I was tired and didn't have the strength to stop my brain from trying to work things out or replaying old events.

I increasingly realised that alcohol wasn't the answer; neither were my other forms of self-hate, but going to God just seemed to put a penny in the slot that opened the floodgates. I knew He wanted to hold me and keep me safe, but I couldn't allow myself to go to Him. Something was stopping me and seemed to want me to be isolated.

Driving in my car were the times where it was just me and God. I could shout, cry and pour out my heart to Him. I felt like a ball of wool - not a neatly tied up one but an unravelling one - and if I were to describe myself as a colour, it would be a mucky brown. If I were to be knitted up, it would be an old-fashioned dishcloth that certainly didn't do the job it was intended to do. Oh, to be a beautiful, cream, Aran cardigan and not a flimsy half-squeezed-out dishcloth! My music was turned up to twenty-one, so it was a good job Geoff didn't know! "You'll ruin the speakers!" he always said and would promptly turn it down to fourteen. I think it was more likely to be the 'old man' creeping up on him rather than concern for the speakers!

As I cried out to God, I asked Him to put me all back together to what I was created to be. At that moment, out of the music jumped the words, *"You don't belittle us in our pain and our suffering, but You comfort us in our greatest unravelling."* I'd never noticed those words before. "Oh, Father!" I sensed my walls melting and felt Him close to me. "Wow, God! How do you do that?" I marvelled at the preciseness of how and when He speaks. He sees me, He hears me and never stops acting on my behalf. Although we only sometimes see His hand move, rest-assured, He never stops, He never sleeps, and I AM His priority. It always makes me laugh that everyone is His priority! How is that possible? Yet He stops and sees and hears me! Oh the Fathering of God that His attention is across the Earth yet His eyes gaze on me and I can have His full attention!

A few weeks passed by and there had been some strong victories and some smaller ones, too. My feelings seemed entrenched, and I was explaining to Ann, one day, how it felt like there was a blockage or giant that I couldn't seem to get over but I didn't even know what it was. She had *that look*. Oh dear! That look! This meant she wanted to suggest something but wasn't sure how I would react. I wasn't sure what she was going to say so I reacted by closing my eyes for a moment, put my hands over my mouth and felt my heart race! "I've not done something wrong have I?" That was always my first question; I defaulted to assuming that everything was my fault.

"No, of course not. Pippa, we have a very good longstanding friend; in fact, he was the minister that married Rob and I all those years ago. My eyes tightened and I clenched my fists. I could tell where this was leading, and I wasn't happy. I definitely didn't want to talk to anyone else and didn't want to have to repeat the horrid things I'd said to Rob and Ann. She continued, "Steve Hepden sometimes speaks at the Restoration Centre in Stockport and holds healing sessions for traumatised, damaged people. He really is someone you can trust and has insight that might be helpful to us."

"Ohhh, I'm really not sure!" I said with an angry, stubborn feeling inside that I didn't want to show Ann because I knew that all she wanted was to help. In that moment, I felt angry at God. All those things that happened to me weren't my choice and now I was left having to make decisions I didn't want to make and none of it was fair!

Rob walked into the room and could probably tell he'd walked in on a tricky moment. "Rob, tell Pippa about Steve," Ann persisted, attempting it from a different angle.

"Oh, Steve's great!" enthused Rob. "A very kind man with a great sense of humour!" I liked the idea of Steve finding things funny; after all, humour was something that had been instilled in me and, in my opinion, was a great thing to have. I had to trust Rob and Ann's opinion of him and believe it when they said that he may be able to help and that he was trustworthy.

"Anyway, you don't have to say anything you don't want to say; it's up to you," Ann affirmed.

"If I talk to him, please stay with me!"

....

There we were, at the Restoration Centre a few weeks later. To my horror, we ended up on the front row but, thankfully, tucked away on the farthest seat. From the moment the first word was spoken, tears flowed incessantly and, as the worship music continued, it was as if I had been completely stripped bare! All walls came down and nothing at all was hidden. I sobbed and listened to Steve talking about freedom and acceptance. As he talked so naturally and empathetically, I could see the Father's heart! I saw Him weeping over my tears and seeing every pain. As Steve talked about the roots that trauma puts down deep in the soul and about how it stops the child inside from growing healthy and strong, I knew I had to respond and step forward for prayer. I felt so scared and all I could keep repeating was, "Please, Lord, help me to be brave. Help me to be brave!"

To my astonishment, Steve came over to pray for me, gently put his face next to mine and whispered into my ear, "You were such a brave little girl. And now I see you being very, very brave. You endured so much, and you tried to keep smiling. The pain was so big, and no little girl should have to deal with that level of hurt and pain."

I felt so touched that my Father had seen me smiling even when I was hurting and the fact that God thought I was brave, melted me. I had always felt I'd been brave, but nobody ever knew the bravery I'd have to maintain, which hurt. But here, right now, God saw, and I felt He was proud of me.

Over the next few weeks, my emotions needed time to calm but, running parallel, there was fruit which was becoming evident: I was becoming braver and more confident. Normally, Geoff would have to drive me whenever I had to go somewhere different, but now I found myself going on my own without a second thought. I also shocked myself to realise I was able to disagree with someone (kindly, of course) without fear of what they thought. I realised that if God valued me so much, I must value the life He'd given me. Irrespective of how hard it was to trust in the future, I had to keep surrendering everything I was to Him who sacrificed everything for me.

As I left the Restoration centre weeks before, I'd had Steve's words resounding in my head; "Don't stay at the crossroads for long!" It was said out of love, and I was increasingly aware that it was going to have to be a lifelong surrender. I was starting to walk the right walk and had to try not to keep changing roads. Oh, I wished there was a 'diversion' sign at the wrong roads to guide me... but that's the Holy Spirits job! I just needed to listen and obey.

How grateful I am that the steadfast love of the Lord never changes, that His mercies never come to an end and every morning they are new. The Lord wasn't bringing my fragmented heart back together but He was giving me a completely NEW one. I'd not really understood the term 'disassociation' and hadn't really acknowledged the need to be healed from the 'escape' state of mind I'd gone into during the trauma but one thing I knew: He would give me clarity of mind and connect all my feelings, body, soul and spirit. I longed for the bringing together of the wounded child and the adult.

"How is she doing?" Steve asked, one evening. I didn't really want Ann to tell him that I was doing well then doing badly then ok then not so good. I wanted him to be proud of my progress but because of my inconsistency, I felt embarrassed. His sense of humour delivered an answer which made me laugh but was so true! Sometimes we are like a Blackpool donkey when we are healing: up and down! It is normal and it is ok!

It was becoming so evident that the little girl inside needed encouragement and to be given a voice. I was starting to find myself being mindful of her and every time I felt she was hurting, I asked for God's help to comfort her. In a strange new way, I was feeling more in control and able to let the lost little girl's feelings go because I felt safer and not alone.

I started to think about the letter I wrote when I was a little girl: such a desperate and sad plea! As a little girl, I believed that the only person who could read it was God and knew that there was nothing I could do to stop it all tumbling out once I'd started to write. I felt brave and because I believed that no one else would see it, the fear, the honesty and the desperate petitions came out thick and fast. As I wrote, I had a fantasy that someone was going to read it and I would be rescued. Now seemed the right time to write back to little Pippa and answer her letter but this time, I would write from the best and most healing perspective: God's... hand in hand with mine, the adult Pippa.

The brave yet fragile little girl was growing up and the strength in me felt good. It was now time to adjust and build up my emotional stamina. Sometimes, it felt like things were going too fast as although I was changing and could see growth and maturity in how I handled things, I would also suddenly find myself panicking because an old feeling or reaction would jump up out of the blue. It was all part of God strengthening me and the "Blackpool Donkey" analogy mode such sense!

We'd planned another trip to Stockport to see Steve and fill him in on the progress. Rob came as well as it was chance for him to catch up, too. Upon arrival, Steve slipped a small piece of paper into my hand and when I had a moment, I uncurled the paper. It read: *Faith is a choice we make and a position we hold!* How relevant was this quote and how helpful it has been on my journey!

We met in a local farm shop cafe which was rather quaint yet felt a little bizarre due to the subject matter we were about to discuss. Armed with scrambled egg on toast, two Cumberland sausages and generous helpings of brown sauce (on Steve's recommendation), we all tucked in! The conversation flowed quite well but I had to keep escaping to the toilet to take a deep breath as my anxiety levels were up a little due to the fact that I didn't know what Steve would ask me next. So far so good, I was thinking, but then Steve suggested we went a stroll around the farm's pig pens and fields, housing llamas that looked rather suspicious; they stood so still without even flickering an eyelid!

Steve has a few difficulties walking so promptly asked me if I minded him holding on to me. Linking arms, he held my hand, too. To anyone else, this would seem a perfectly normal thing to do but, for me, it was too close and too personal considering the things we were trying to casually talk about. Ann and Rob kept a watchful and wary eye on me and prayed for me in tongues under their breath, knowing how I must be feeling. I gritted my teeth and pushed down those feelings, completely out of my comfort zone. I felt unsafe and was completely unable to say so for two reasons: I did not have it within me to be so rude and the fear that gripped me made the small child rise up, making it almost impossible to say, "No!" I was so angry with myself that this still raised its ugly head when put in such a position, making it impossible for me to do such a simple thing!

Leaning against the fence, Steve asked if we could pray. To my astonishment, as he prayed, something was happening inside. I felt a release from fear and, suddenly, my legs gave way and I crumbled to the floor. It could have been so embarrassing as the general public were also strolling round the farm but all that mattered to me was that God was setting me free and, at that moment, I felt so loved. As I got up off the floor, brushing off the gravel and debris, I looked at Steve and felt so deeply grateful that he had held my hand and seen me through another part of learning to trust and see God come in to father me.

....

I couldn't escape or hide from the love of God. He was always on my case and, no sooner had one issue been tackled, challenged and released, He would gently lead me into the next. A prophet from South Africa, Gebhardt Bernt, was visiting a local church and Geoff had been to a couple of the meetings where God had spoken clearly to him. Ann gently encouraged me to go to the next meeting and I quickly shied away from that idea. I had this strange notion that if Gebhardt heard God clearly, which I didn't doubt at all, then he would see all the mess inside me and I couldn't stand that. I felt too fragile and wanted to hide away, especially from a Man of God who I deeply admired, because I felt I fell so far short of where I thought I should be.

However, there I was again... somehow on the front row! There were no chairs and I desperately tried to push backwards, to no avail. Oh dear, here we go again! I could feel the pull on my heart again. I was trying so hard to hold it all together, but I knew I was in the presence of God, and I really had nothing to lose but to be open. Gebhardt and his team began to pray for me with such accuracy! God had got my attention!

Eric prayed first. "You have taken a lot of blows and a lot of things have come against you, but God says you are a strong, brave woman and you mustn't be afraid to speak. You are going to be like an ant hill where many, many people will come to you and take from you, and you will be a refuge for many."

Gebhardt immediately took over: "You have difficulties with your speech and expressing yourself and God is releasing you now. He is releasing you from shame and fear, too. This night." He went on to whisper in my ear, "I see demons coming

146

in the night and whispering lies to you. Tonight, I am removing the memories, oh the memories! I release peace over your mind, and I unblock your ears and eyes to see from God's perspective." He went on to say, "I see you as a very little girl, maybe six years old, and you were powerless. I release you from being muddled and I release your true self to shine because what you've been through and learnt is what others need. I cut off you deep disappointment and the constant fear of failure and God says He will not allow you to debase yourself to feel you are of lower status or to belittle your quality and character." He went on to say that he saw me with lots of grandchildren and that I would die as an old lady despite always believing that I would die young. "Pippa, you have a damaged wing, but you are a big eagle, and, from this day, you will fly healed."

The next bit was a difficult one as Gebhardt asked me about myself and, up to that point, he hadn't known me at all. It always made me really anxious giving away really personal details to people I didn't know well. He said that the blockage I felt was a spirit causing trauma and he could see it sitting in my womb area. "Could I release it, Pippa?" he asked, kindly.

"Yes please!" I answered with huge relief, marvelling again at God's gentle way. He began to pray and, after three spirits were released, my body felt limp and totally relaxed. I chuckled silently to myself as Gebhardt said, "Hang on; a bit of trauma is hiding but I can see it. Out, in Jesus' name!" I felt a surge up through my stomach and, with the fourth burp, it was out, and I was free! Rather a strange happening to some but for me, it made total sense that the fears we collect along our journey of life sit deep within us and fear causes physical reactions. So, the physical feeling of it leaving was a sure sign that it was out and that's the clarity God gives. He's a thorough, all-knowing and gentle God!

Steve's curled up paper with the words *'Faith is a choice I make and a position I hold'* certainly helped me focus during the coming months, to cement and keep hold of all the healing God had done.

Chapter Eighteen
Who Dares Wins

Oh no! My Uncle Dick had died and that meant only one thing... another family funeral and another encounter with Uncle Ivan! During my childhood, I'd not had much to do with Uncle Dick because my mum had said that he had an 'unsavoury' lifestyle. As the years unfolded, I realised that she hadn't been wrong. The stories of his exploits fascinated me, yet my mother's quotation from the Bible, 'Come out from among them and be separate' made total sense. Guns, post offices, get away cars and night-time shopping when all the shops were shut were his everyday language. He was a very handsome man and very suave, slicking his dark hair back regularly with his comb that was a permanent fixture in his back pocket. He was the 'mafia' in his hometown.

As soon as I was old enough, I wanted more than anything to tell him about Jesus. My mum had tried but, with her sincere Methodist approach, they never quite connected; they were a thousand miles apart. I used to chuckle to myself and say, "I wonder why!"

I, on the other hand, could somehow see how much potential there was in him, and I could see how much God loved him. His way of thinking didn't put me off but rather drove me to pray for him more and be determined to introduce him to the saving grace of Jesus, who I knew full well forgave all our sins.

I was sixteen when I had the opportunity to share my faith with him. It was like a veil pulled back and he saw the truth of the salvation that Jesus offers everyone. Over several months,

Uncle Dick, Geoff and I would go along to church and every time was eventful as he began to look anew at the way he was living, and it challenged him to the core. We could see underneath all his bravado and macho persona that he was softening towards God. Unfortunately, he eventually, and with deep sadness, could not grasp hold of what was on offer to him and he returned to his criminal lifestyle.

I always wanted to tell Uncle Dick about Uncle Ivan. Even though he was like he was, somehow I trusted him. He used to grab me and hold me and say, "Tha's beautiful; I love thee," and always followed on by saying, "If anyone hurts you, Pippa, I will kill them!" Knowing his reputation, I knew it was possible!

A text landed to say that Uncle Dick had died. It felt like all my 'good' uncles, or rather the ones who never hurt me, were dead but the one who still hurt me was still living. In addition, I still had to see him, and Auntie Glenda continued to talk freely about him, thinking nothing of strolling through photos that included him and shoving them under my nose. 'This is it,' I thought to myself. 'I've got to tell her; I've got to get through to her that things MUST change!'

....

Pippa, Uncle Ivan and I are coming to the funeral; can I stay with you for a few days? The text came through and I didn't answer for a while. I didn't feel like having to pamper to her insecurities again. The last few months had been such an emotional time; the thought of it depressed me. What choice did I have? Geoff had got used to having her stay, regardless of his frustrations over her neediness. From past experience, he knew it was pointless disagreeing with me as I couldn't and wouldn't upset her and certainly hadn't wanted to upset Mum when she'd been alive.

"Ok, Auntie Glenda, but I'm afraid you can only stay for one night." She was displeased but that was the only offer on the table, so she accepted it. Maybe it was time to bring up the subject of fresh boundaries and maybe, just maybe, she would talk with me about the past and how Uncle Ivan's actions have affected me!

It was no good going into this without my trusted friend, Ann. I never really felt like I could fully express myself and how on earth could I say such dreadful stuff to my uncle's wife! Who could? Ann posed the question of what it was that I wanted from this 'talk'.

"Well, I need her to understand that after the funeral I never want to see him again or hear his voice in the background while she is on the phone or see any photos of him. For me to be able to move on, this is necessary."

So, we hatched a plan; well, it was sort of a plan. After all, we weren't sure how it would work out or even if I'd have the guts to do it. "Pippa, I won't say anything you don't want me to but, equally, whatever you want me to say, I'm happy to say it. Just give me a nod. You take the lead."

....

My heart was racing although to all intents and purposes, no one would have suspected anything. Auntie and I were sitting chatting happily and a knock came at the door. "Who's that? Who are you expecting?" I answered the door and Ann walked in with cream cakes and a smile that gave nothing away.

"Oh Auntie, this is my friend, Ann, and she's going to stay a while for a cuppa." Auntie Glenda was not happy as she had always been the jealous type, demanding my sole attention and if she saw me being close and complimentary towards another friend, it seemed to threaten her place in my friendship hierarchy. Oh boy! We went round in circles chatting about something and nothing but as time passed, I knew it was building to a point where I would just have to launch into it. And launch I did!

"Auntie Glenda I want to talk to you." Her demeanour instantly changed. "I really, really don't want to upset you, but I have to talk to you about Uncle Ivan and how he still affects me." I tried to speak in a non-threatening, kind voice but I don't think it would have mattered how I presented it. Auntie Glenda was immediately a mixture of angry and defensive and didn't seem to have an ounce of empathy for what I'd suffered.

"What is she doing here?" Auntie demanded to know, with venom in her voice! She thrust her finger at Ann, "And why on earth are you talking in front of her? She's got nothing to do with it!"

"Yes, she has!" I retorted quickly. "Actually, Ann knows everything!"

Before I could explain, poor Ann was subjected to Auntie Glenda's full wrath. She shouted at her like a crazed woman! "You know nothing! I've known Pippa all her life so what have you got to do with anything?"

Ann replied in a calm but firm voice, "Actually, Glenda, Pippa has talked to me about Uncle Ivan and it's important that you understand how and why she is continuing to struggle with this. Pippa is the victim and needs all the support we can give."

Auntie was furious. "I'M a victim; I'M innocent, too! What about me in all this? I've done nothing wrong and why on earth is this thing being brought up again?"

I tried to explain that this was the last thing I ever wanted to do but I needed her to understand what I had gone through. I went on to explain how I'd found such a good friend in Ann and I trusted her implicitly, valuing her judgment, her honesty and how sincere she had been in helping me try to work through my struggles. While I was explaining, I suddenly had a moment of honesty and bravery and said, "Actually, Auntie Glenda, Ann's husband Rob knows everything too." I squinted my eyes as I knew it wouldn't be a pretty reaction.

She sat bolt upright and, as if I'd done the worst of crimes, shouted, "You're joking!"

"No, I'm not. I needed his help, too." I explained how it wasn't always easy talking to Geoff as he was too emotionally involved but I needed a man's perspective - one I could trust and be brutally honest with.

"What on earth have you said? This is too much for me; you're going to kill me... and Uncle Ivan is old, now. How will we ever get over this?" Without a breath in between sentences, she launched into a barrage of questions asking for details of what happened, where and for how long. This was the thing I was dreading, and I had no idea how I would navigate through it. As I began to give her some insight, she cut across and said, "Well, where was I? How did he get time to do this?"

"I don't know where you were when it happened, Auntie. He's a manipulator and he picked his moments carefully." I explained some events in detail which she acknowledged as true because she remembered the awful confrontation years before and remembered Uncle Ivan's acknowledgement, at the time, of the dreadful series of events.

By this stage, Auntie looked awful, and I felt awful! I couldn't help but go and sit on the floor at her feet and try to hold her hands.

"Oh, Auntie! We will get through this!"

Ann calmly said, "Let's try and bring this back to why we are talking about this. Glenda, you have to understand and do what's needed for Pippa to heal."

"Well, what's that?" Auntie snapped with disdain.

Ann went on to explain how it was important that I never had to ever see him again and that seeing photos of him was really upsetting for me so that mustn't happen either.

"There have been times, Auntie, when you've FaceTimed me on your phone and he's in the background or I can hear him!"

Ann piped up quickly as Auntie jumped to defend herself again: "You don't seem to understand how much this has affected Pippa."

Suddenly out of the blue, Auntie's voice changed. She looked up, grabbed her iPad and, as though we were casually discussing what was on the news, brightly said, "Would you like to hear a poem?" She launched into it as Ann looked at me in astonishment!

"Well...erm...go on then," I replied, wondering why on earth we were having to listen to a poem when we were in the middle of a serious and distressing conversation about child abuse! I guess it showed her mental instability and her detachment from the seriousness of the reality she was facing.

I then made a mistake – well, it seems like it was, looking back at it. Auntie looked so upset and I was very concerned that what we were talking about was too challenging and was going to make her ill. She certainly looked it, so, I tried for a moment to make her feel that I wasn't putting all the blame on Uncle Ivan. I disclosed to her that others had hurt me in similar ways. She latched onto that immediately and it almost seemed as though she transferred all her anger towards them, thus shifting focus completely off Uncle Ivan. She was livid that other people had hurt me and repeatedly asked me who they were and if she knew them. When I said that one was a Christian in church, she verbally exploded and, with absolute acidity in her voice, blasted, "Christians! Such hypocrites!"

I quickly jumped to the defence of Christians and said that she seemed to be missing the point; plus, that was ONE Christian's actions, which were so wrong, but she didn't ought to tar us all with the same brush as there were many genuine ones who wouldn't dream of doing such a thing.

Ann was keen to bring the conversation back round to the reasons we had brought it up. She clarified, again, that my need was to be protected and that Auntie must do that. Auntie Glenda sort of acknowledged it but quickly went on to say how on earth could she not talk about him and what if she made a mistake? "I can't help being married to him!" She swore and it was very clear that she was deeply angry at Uncle Ivan: angry at him for what he'd done and angry at what he'd caused. She couldn't seem to separate her desire to help me from her own desperate feelings of his betrayal and the consequences she found herself having to face. I could see that, and my heart hurt beyond belief for her. I wasn't angry with her as I knew that what I had said must have caused her deep pain. I could see that she genuinely knew nothing at the time that it was happening and the one thing she did say, which was healing to hear, was that had she walked in on him hurting me, she would have gone berserk and thrown him out.

It was getting very late, and we were all extremely tired, although none of us would have been able to sleep. The adrenaline was still coursing around my body, and I was wondering how on earth we could bring this horrendous night to an acceptable conclusion.

Then, Auntie struck up with the next wave of conflict. "So, who else knows? If your other Aunties and Uncles knew, it would kill me! What about our children? Oh no... what if he's done it to my daughter! Oh no... what about my granddaughter!" All these questions rolled out of her mouth but, fortunately, without much of a gap for me to answer. At that moment, I was so thankful to God that no actual response seemed to be required as I knew, and Ann knew, that others DID know, and other family members knew. At that moment, if I would have had to be honest and tell her, I think she would have verbally annihilated me!

It had been the worst of evenings and, although I guess I'd managed to express my need and made my expectations clear, I still felt sad, sorry and guilty for putting Auntie Glenda through this. Ann left and Auntie was staying the night, so I kindly encouraged her to bed and pointed out that tomorrow was a new day.

After a rather troubled night (and, I guess, Auntie's was too), I greeted her with trepidation as she appeared the next morning. She burst forth into a troubled conversation. I couldn't blame her as she'd gone to bed so late, having to deal with such difficult information. It was no wonder she had questions bursting to come out.

"Why on earth did you go back for more when you were older, knowing what had happened previously?"

"Auntie, I had no choice! I'd tried to say that I hadn't wanted to go but, by that point, I was too compliant and was scared to say anything – I'd just desperately hoped that he wouldn't do anything again. I had wanted to believe that he wouldn't dare to try to repeat it!"

I certainly don't think she accepted my explanation. She quickly moved on to threaten me with the words, "If you've told anyone else, I will hang myself!" I gulped as I knew that I had! I wasn't going to tell her, though!

We talked for some time, but it wasn't constructive and in no shape or form was it about me; it became all about her needs, her feelings and nothing I said could change that. Auntie Glenda was in no state to leave as we'd planned, so I reluctantly asked her to stay one more night to calm her a little before she went and entered her next battle. I felt truly sorry for her and so sad that I'd brought up such a painful thing.

The day was tense and emotional, and my mind and emotions felt shattered. I felt like she looked at me differently. I felt dirty, like I'd betrayed her, but couldn't help feeling that she had betrayed me a little too by questioning me as if what I did was wrong.

We got through the day and the following morning seemed to arrive so slowly. I just wanted it all over yet I wanted us to part with an understanding that this was hard on both sides, but we still loved each other. I needed to reaffirm to her what I wanted from this but somehow, I didn't think she'd got it as she continued to refer to him but not by name.

So, Evie stepped in. She is passionate for justice, and she is a great communicator, so this felt right. Evie is my eldest and, up until this point, she had fully respected my wishes by not tackling the issue with Auntie Glenda, but she looked in my eyes and said, "Mum, I'm going to talk to her! She MUST understand what you need, and I will make it clear to her. No reference to him, no photos of him and no more visits from him!" I agreed and felt a big relief as I knew she could do a better job of it than me.

Evie was shocked by what she heard. Auntie Glenda had said, without any build up or context, "Why did Pippa not have someone with her at all times?"

"What a crazy thing to say!" I said. "IF ONLY!" And then Evie lowered her tone and said how Auntie had gone on to say in a firm, cocky voice, "Well, Evie, it wasn't just Uncle Ivan who did stuff to your mum; there were three others too!" It was almost like she was diluting what Uncle Ivan had done. Evie quickly responded by saying how irrelevant that was in this situation and it didn't alter the seriousness of what Uncle Ivan did. I felt hurt that Auntie could so easily share that with Evie. I had naively presumed that she would have wanted to protect my children from information like that.

One thing was clear: even though she'd fiercely defended herself and tried to minimise Uncle Ivan's actions, he was, without a doubt, going to get the full wrath of Auntie Glenda when they got home. That gave me a huge conflicting mix of emotions as I felt really concerned about how he would react. Would he be angry at me? I had spoken to Auntie about it all despite saying to Uncle that I wouldn't, so I'd broken my word. Maybe he would ban Auntie from seeing me again!

One thing I knew for certain was that Geoff, my children and my closest friends loved me and knew my heart. Above it all, I belonged to Jesus and throughout all the years, He had never left me or failed to bring me through my difficulties. So, my resolve was set, to trust Him.

Auntie left. We hugged and tried our best to smile at each other but both of us knew our relationship was damaged and I was uncertain as to what would happen in the future.

The day of Uncle Dick's funeral arrived. Would Uncle Ivan be there? Would Auntie have said anything? Surely, he won't be there! I was desperately hoping not.

Geoff and I arrived early. I wanted to catch up with my cousins and family that I hadn't seen for a long time... and there he was! The moment I saw him, I squeezed Geoff's hand so tightly. I felt sick and knew I had to be really strong and really brave regardless of what he did or said. Geoff and I agreed a plan: he would stay with me at all times, and he was to keep his eye on wherever Uncle Ivan was.

After ten minutes of chatting, Geoff was absorbed with family who were catching up on each other's news and I found myself a few feet away from him. He'd seen me and had started to make his way towards me. He looked serious and stern, and I knew that Auntie Glenda had definitely spoken to him. My heart started to thump, and my mouth went dry but, from somewhere, a strength rose up within me and, as he came close, I completely turned my back on him, giving him a clear message - I WASN'T talking. He tried to intimidate me throughout the whole service by not taking his eyes off me, but I stayed strong and just gently prayed to Jesus under my breath. A new 'me' was emerging! Not only had I turned my back, I'd refused to engage in conversation and I'd refused to respond to his intimidation tactics. I was now an adult who could make my own choices and I could protect myself without feeling guilty. Out of the blue, he brushed past me and looked me straight in my eyes as he made a spitting sound and I saw such disdain in his eyes. This was the first time I'd ever seen him like this, and it helped me to see that he really wasn't sorry or ashamed of what he'd done but was angry at me for my response... and the control he had held for so long was now in my hands. I wasn't hiding his secret anymore. I had dared to stand up to him and I felt I'd won.

Chapter Nineteen
The Kiss of Heaven

There is only one kiss that brings to life the broken soul: a kiss so sweet and so pure.

My heart is like a walled garden, it is a secret place for me and Jesus, the lover of my soul. No one else can enter that place but it's so easy to leave it unattended and the weeds grow up, the vines wind round, and soon, you couldn't even find it even if you looked.

This place I knew so well and had entered every day as a little girl, but I had somehow got so lost along the way. Oh, I loved Him and, oh, how I wanted to please Him, but I had forgotten that secret, secret place. Jesus, the lover of my heart had been held at a distance and I hadn't even noticed.

In the beginning, I didn't need to surrender or to lay anything down; He had my heart, He dwelled with me, and we often didn't need words; after all, they were flawed and incomplete. His glance, His eyes lit my heart and I'd felt so deeply loved.

Where had all that gone? I had slowly covered myself with shame and self-loathing and I'd started to not recognise who He really was. The men that hurt me had kissed me with death; I had started to hide who I was and had lost who I was. The Jesus that my Daddy had introduced me to had given me true identity but, as a small child, that identity had been distorted and it had been tormented by lies even though I thought I was living in truth.

I was realising that the secret crucible of my heart had been overtaken by my fears and my ideas, and I had made my struggles matter more than what mattered most.

Even when I wanted to change, it was as if I couldn't; a level of freedom would come but then another issue would creep in. The house you build is the dwelling you end up living in and, in builders' language, I'd had a cowboy builder on site, and he'd done a bodge job. As it says in the Bible, 'Unless the Lord builds the house, we labour in vain."

If ever I realised the importance of daily putting on the armour of God, it was now. Satan so desperately wanted to snatch away the work of God in my life, and there was only one person who could stop that happening... me. The armour of God hasn't been given to every Christian to be worn 'as and when' but to be a daily dressing. The helmet of salvation isn't just to remind you that Jesus has saved you once but it's to cover your mind in the daily knowledge that this salvation has become personal and it washes you, covers you, renews you and transforms you. The shield of faith needs to be held firmly and intentionally, as it distinguishes every fiery dart that the enemy of our souls fires against us. We can, by faith, withstand anything that comes against us, and we can protect our hearts; after all, our heart is precious and soft, and we need to protect it as the King dwells there. The breastplate of righteousness wasn't something that I could earn or attain but was a piece of the armour that had been paid for by Jesus. He had become my righteousness and He freely gave me this part of equipment to wear in faith knowing that if I slip and fall, His righteous character covers me.

I was increasingly realising that the belt of truth needed strapping on daily and I knew full well that without living in the truth, my life felt as good as over. No matter how distorted things feel, or perceptions become, there is only one truth that holds firm and cannot be moved or altered: Jesus. He is the Way, the Truth and the Life, and my life is hidden in Him, so I can face all the enemy's lies without them affecting me. I'm not the sum total of what life has done to me or what I feel. I am so meticulously crafted and, to make it even better, it is in my Heavenly Father's image.

The final part of the armour is around the 'feet department', as my mother always put it. Shoes made with the gospel of peace. What a beautiful thing that wherever you go or whatever you have to walk through, the gospel of peace is with you. I always imagine all the different sized feet people have, but the pair of shoes that God gives us are not picked off any random shelf. They are made by the Master shoemaker and cobbler. The shoemaker has them perfectly sized and fitted whilst as the Master cobbler too, He does all the repairs that are needed. We should all walk round in the gospel of peace and not just for ourselves but to give it away.

I was struggling to fully let go and was aware of an area that needed tackling... and it wasn't pretty! It was embarrassing and humiliating but I needed to get my head around the fear of part of the anatomy - the male one. Yikes! How would we deal with this one? First of all, I'd spent years trying to not upset Geoff about it and certainly didn't feel it appropriate to talk to anyone else about it.

I'd had a run of several days where I couldn't get out of my head the fact that men had a deadly weapon, and it was an impossibility to put that weapon and love in the same sentence.

Dare I open up to Rob and Ann? I'd mentioned it in the past and I felt that now was the time to get rid of it, but what on earth would they think of me and how on earth could I say it? Ann encouraged me, saying, "There's no time like the present so let's nip it in the bud," in her schoolteacher / mum voice!

"Right!" I paused. "If I share this, first of all, Rob, I'm taking a great risk trusting you as you come under the category of 'men' and I don't want you thinking anything or feeling anything negative or bad towards me so, while I'm talking, I'm imagining you're not Rob but rather Roberta. It was becoming a standard joke as poor old Rob was getting used to his new role. The thoughts of him not sitting there as a man but simply a friend, seemed to help.

The laughter lightened the atmosphere as we thrashed through how past experiences shouldn't tar every man with the same brush. Rob said that the real issue wasn't that every man *has* one, which makes him a potential threat, but rather it's the *intent*. All men have the anatomy but only a few have the intent to harm. Although it made sense, it was a battle of wills as I had an underlying distrust of men and almost a stubbornness against being willing to change; there was a real inward fight between the fears and the truth. I physically felt a ripping feeling begin to start inside my chest and I didn't sleep well that night. The heaviness and sense of tearing in my chest was almost unbearable. I couldn't navigate through it and, although I cried out to God to show me what was happening, nothing happened. I felt the most anxious I'd ever felt, like I'd unearthed a dreadful thing.

How on earth could I carry on? I wasn't living; where was this abundant life that God so easily gives? The truth of the matter was that I'd listened to lies for so long, I'd given them a home. It was time to move past any blame on other people's part; I had to take responsibility for what I'd taken on and how I'd nurtured the wrong views and taken on an identity that God never intended for me.

It came to mind, from years ago, that a little wispy old lady had come over to me after a church service one evening and said, someone has kissed you with a kiss that's brought death, but Jesus wants to kiss you back to life.

And here I am, all these years later, still harbouring death when, all along, my Jesus has been waiting for me. How unbelievable and stupid had I behaved and what crazy choices I'd made! It had grown deep in me a default setting that set everything back to escape and hiding mode whenever faced with a trigger.

....

The following Sunday morning, I went to church. Figuratively speaking, I was kicking and screaming inside. The anxiety was through the roof, my emotional pain was physical, and I felt all the demons of hell against me. It didn't help that I now wanted to escape and couldn't. Hiding wasn't an option because God stood in front of me and, as I turned, He was behind me; in fact, He utterly surrounded me. There was no place to hide, there was no thought hidden and no lies had a leg to stand on. I knew, in that moment, two things He wanted me to do. Firstly, He simply asked me to hold His hand.

I felt so tiny and small and fragile, and I said, "Daddy, my Father, please take hold of my hand," and it slipped into the warmest, most loving hand. His hand revealed His heart. I can barely write about it! The tenderness and purity of His heart was like liquid that poured through His hand to me. I looked up into His eyes. Oh, His eyes! I remember them so well. The first thing I saw when I looked into them was who I was. It was like a seamlessness. Creation's intention of union between a child and her Father. Identity was never made to be an issue. My identity had *never* been in question. Oh, what a fearsome thing that is to Satan. He has NO identity; he has been stripped of his name. His eternal home only holds fear and separation, his disobedience cost him everything and the only light he knows is death. The enemy of my soul desperately wanted to take me with him. Unknowingly, I'd come into agreement with the lies, becoming a partner of them. There are only two voices, and the shepherd of my heart was calling me back to the place called home.

Returning to the garden of my heart could never have been described as an escape; after all, I was running into it and not away from it. I'd heard it said so many times that people turn to church as a crutch but, oh, how wrong they are. To find that secret place is a gift and, in trying to get away from the pain, I was actually getting further away from the only place where I could truly become whole.

As I knew without a shadow of a doubt that my Heavenly Father was holding my hand, I felt safe again; safe from pain and fear, and the second thing that I knew He was wanting from me was surrender... and that meant *everything*. Surrender is to submit to a higher power who has authority above your own, and yielding is not about bending under duress, but rather not being hard and rigid. I had become both of those things: hardening myself from the tender love of God and become rigid in the opinions of myself, refusing to believe I could be forgiven and truly changed.

Oh, the peace that flowed into my mind. It was instant and, immediately, I could see a vision of all the anguish that I had carried... a minute fraction of the world's anguish that was laid upon the Lord's chest as He suffered innocently for us. In a moment, I found myself asking for a fraction of the weight of people's anguish to remain as I never wanted to forget what people carried or to forget the full provision that He made to bear it.

The battle throughout my life wasn't to prove I was right or to be the one who conquered the uncles and bad people in my life; it wasn't even just to be the winner. The battle was to live in the beauty Jesus has created! People along the way get it terribly wrong and some make evil choices against us, but we shouldn't focus on fighting them. Rather, we must focus on the enemy of our souls and make sure the door of our hearts is firmly shut to him. It is only the Lord that should indwell our hearts and He is the one who heals us and completes us.

The wobbles and the setbacks are not an indicator of the true work that has taken place. Reminders and triggers are gradually replaced by new memories, and old, destructive feelings by positive ones. New patterns of thinking take time - and lots of it - and it takes strength, good choices and gritted teeth not to want to keep returning to what seems natural.

Our Father in Heaven has one thing on His mind: our full attention! Hiding is part and parcel of how we protect ourselves from abuse, which is a normal self-protection, but the truth far outweighs the rationale of the broken mind. We don't have to hide ourselves from God; after all, He sees everything and lays it bare! He is one we can trust without exception.

I have a thousand more things I could say and still more healing needs to take place and be cemented in me, but I have finally found myself in a beautiful God-given place that says: I am loved, I am listened to and I am valued. I always was, but didn't realise it until now, and nothing can change the truth of my future.

Across my path, people are coming who are walking the walk I was lost in, and I want to take them in my arms and share the wonderful love of Jesus that has so tenderly healed me.

I can see the 'golden squares' and, just as I was so broken, I will take each one and love them, listen to them and value them.

Epilogue

As the waves keep rolling in, the tide, in its time, goes out. This is how my story develops and evolves.

As the old patterns and thoughts change and slowly move away to be left in my past, new waves come, bringing challenges that I hadn't seen before. I guess this is not the conclusion of the story; in fact, it's just the beginning. I would like to say that every sadness and trace of damage is gone but, in actual fact, I'm walking in new shoes that need bedding in. There will be more challenges and adjustments to make but the one thing I know for certain is that I am not alone and, if you have a similar story, neither are you. The promise that Jesus gives us, stands. He will perfect that which concerns me... and that is true for you, too.

The story doesn't end here. Should such crimes against a child be buried? Does forgiveness mean forgetting and not confronting?

The new book coming out soon (She's Seen, She's heard and She's safe) covers these issues and takes the reader on the complex journey involving the Police and Crime Prosecution Service.

BV - #0038 - 160524 - C0 - 229/152/9 - PB - 9781913181772 - Matt Lamination